VALUE INVESTING
TODAY

VALUE INVESTING TODAY

Charles H. Brandes

IRWIN
Professional Publishing®
Chicago • London • Singapore

To L.F.B.

Project editor: Margaret Haywood
Production manager: Ann Cassady
Jacket design: Mike Finkelman
Compositor: TCSystems, Inc.
Typeface: 11/13 Century Schoolbook
Printer: R. R. Donnelley & Sons Company

Library of Congress Cataloging-in-Publication Data
Brandes, Charles H.
    Value investing today/by Charles H. Brandes.
       p.   cm.
    Includes index.
    ISBN 1-55623-178-4
    1. Stocks. 2. Investments. I. Title.
HG4661.B68   1989
332.6'78—dc20   89–31621
                             CIP

Printed in the United States of America
8 9 0 DO 6

PREFACE

There are two points that I would like to make clear. First, this is not a book of stock "winners." For that you will have to seek elsewhere.

The second point is this: The specific shares mentioned in this book and all descriptions of the corporate backgrounds affecting them are given solely as a means of making the basic value principles that I am attempting to explain, more clear and, I hope, more interesting. None of the information is furnished as a recommendation to buy or sell the specific shares.

To those who still cling to so many of the common investment errors that I point out in this book, the record of a quite different investment philosophy is here to read.

Without the help of many people, this book would have remained merely an idea. I gratefully acknowledge their assistance.

W. Roberts Wood, C.F.A., with whom I work, provided the initial spark. Bob steadfastly offered encouragement and support throughout the project.

Likewise, I am indebted to Mary Thode. She edited and proofread the manuscript. Mary kept me from making egregious errors, and any errors that remain are, of course, mine.

Knowing I needed help, Bob, searching for someone with financial and business writing experience, introduced me to John Roaney. John's skill, enthusiasm, and patience were unending. I am indebted for his professional editorial assistance and research.

Finally, I am indebted to my mentor, Benjamin Graham. It was his basic ideas that formed the solid foundations for my thinking.

Time and space do not allow me to mention everyone who helped along the way, including all of my associates.

Charles H. Brandes

CONTENTS

INTRODUCTION

Once upon a time there was an emperor with no clothes. His loyal subjects overlooked this deficiency until one child, casting aside convention and social custom, proclaimed the truth—the emperor wasn't all he'd been cracked up to be.

If you've been involved in the financial world and if you've stood back and observed its machinations thoughtfully, you'll have noticed that there have been many naked emperors. Doubtless, there will be many more.

There is no question that some people will make substantial money by investing in stocks. Others, like the emperor, will lose their shirts. This book is directed toward those investors who know that the worthwhile things in life have to be earned; toward the people who know that quick fixes are likely to be no fixes at all.

The main purpose of this book, then, is to help you take advantage of true investment opportunities by supplying you with the principles of the most successful means of investing over the past 60 years—value investing. I will admit to being a convert to this approach and, as with many converts, I am deeply committed to it. I have seen the results; I know it works; and I know it will build wealth for those who apply its principles. Since this book is not meant as a general overview of investing, I will not be discussing other investment approaches.

A QUICK TOUR . . .

Never before has a book of this nature been so important. Think not? Perhaps a short tour around our investing arena will change your mind.

For several years now individual investors have shaken off the trammels of reason. Instead, they have opted to run wild after golden visions, turning to fads, alchemy, and the stars and moon in desperate efforts to increase their wealth.

Consider the 1960s. Visions of boundless wealth floated before investors from the advent of a new magic formula: *synergy*. Synergy meant that two and two under astute corporate management could indeed equal five.

Synergy was not the first—nor the last—of such gimmicks. We've had go-go stocks, the high-turnover performance game, guessing market cycles and turns, technical analysis, and an infatuation with high technology and new issues. We have also seen the good company/bad price syndrome reappear, as it did in the 1970s, when the so-called nifty-fifty stocks sold at price earnings ratios that reached the sky.

FUNNY MONEY GAMES COMING BACK TO LIFE

In the 1980s we see the reemergence of the old funny money game of the public utility holding companies—financial entrepreneurs using good businesses, such as food companies with established brands, as the base for capital structures so weak as to leave no margin for safety, even for bondholders. We again watch investors exchange stocks at a rate as costly as it is pointless.

Most recently we've had the high debt and junk bond phenomenon. Although different, it is still a circumstance totally lacking in reason and in a sense of history.

Sophisticated investors may snort P.T. Barnum-like remarks directed toward the gullibility of amateur investors and their gypsylike attitude, but they would be wrong.

Amateur investors aren't the only ones at fault. The best and brightest of the financial professionals have proven equally gullible.

Pension funds, insurance companies, and other institutional investors have been abandoning any notion of making a painstaking analysis of the companies whose stocks they buy.[1] Almost uniformly a variety of strategies have been adopted that may differ in some respects but have one horrendous defect in common. They all reject the need or feasibility of making company-by-company judgments about price and value or the need to examine time horizons or other factors that have some relation to the basic fundamentals necessary for long-term *investing.*

SHORT-TERM THINKING NOW IN VOGUE

Near-frenzied trading currently engulfs the securities markets. They have been turned into senior-level Las Vegases. Investors come and go with dazzling frequency. Each of them strives for a larger share of the average annual gains pie; each strives to speed up the process of wealth building. Instead, however, they find themselves switching in and out of different stocks, feeding the brokers instead of themselves.

We have become increasingly preoccupied with short-term events and short-term results. A national impatience has gripped our lives, a trend exacerbated by both the five-year bull market that began in 1982 and ended on October 19, 1987, and its aftermath.

To borrow a few words from Sir John Templeton, a global money manager, there is too much emphasis now in America on everything yesterday. We are no longer as thrifty as we should be, and this is leading to more speculation, more danger, and more risk. Most American investors look too much at the short term, because they think it is so simple to make a right decision that all you need to know is which company is going to have good earnings next year. But it is not as easy as that. As our expectations have increased, our ability to wait and anticipate has decreased. The attention span of most Americans today is about the length of a television show.[2]

This fact applies equally well to the financial world. In Lewis Carroll's classic, *Alice in Wonderland,* Humpty Dumpty says that words mean exactly what he wants them to mean.

Keep this in mind the next time you visit the New York Stock Exchange (NYSE) and listen to the recorded message it has on hand. "Investment objectives," the message relates, "have changed from quick-dollar schemes to savings-oriented vehicles concerned with long-term security."[3]

Have they? Consider that during 1987 at the NYSE more than 35 billion shares switched owners, many switching more than one time. Since 51 billion shares were listed on the NYSE as a whole, nearly three fifths changed hands in a year. Another 28 billion shares were traded in the over-the-counter markets. Add these to the billions traded on the American Stock Exchange.

If stocks are good long-term investments, why aren't they held longer? Despite lip service to long-term investing, investors are encouraged to switch around and chase the latest fad. Although the chase may be exhilarating, it is usually not very profitable.

If investors are to make money consistently, what is required is a return to far-sighted, long-term investing. That is the only kind of investing that promises rational investors the greatest economic rewards over the long haul.

WHAT IS MEANT BY INVESTING?
BY SPECULATION?

Since the investing world currently seems stuck with *Alice in Wonderland* definitions, what is meant by investing? By speculation?

The distinction between investing and speculation has always been difficult to define, even though we understand it well enough in familiar terms. As one turn-of-the-century commentator noted, when a "security is bought and paid for in full, put away in a place of safe keeping, and held for the income it produces—that is called an investment." But, when it "is bought on margin and held for sale as soon as the price advances—that is speculation."[4] I would add: (1) any contemplated holding period shorter than a normal business cycle (three to five years) is speculation, and (2) any purchase based on anticipated market movements or forecasting is also speculation.

This completes our tour. As you can see, a return to proper investing methods today is important . . . no, vital. You will find those methods outlined in *Value Investing Today*.

SUCCESS DEPENDS ON THREE FACTORS

First, let us look at three ingredients necessary for your investing success. As with any endeavor, success depends on three key factors: knowledge, correct action, and patience.

This book supplies the necessary knowledge to guide you toward investments that will help protect and enhance your capital in today's radically changing world. Because of the lightning pace of financial change in the past few years, such a guide is more important now than ever before.

I also spoke of two other key factors: correct action and patience. These you must supply yourself.

The bottom line of value investing, of course, is to make money. If you use the value-investing approach and related tools suggested on the following pages, you should increase your capital, possibly substantially.

VALUE INVESTING TIME-TESTED

Value investing was already enjoying the finest pedigree of any investment strategy when I first learned of it in the early 1970s. At that time I was privileged to become a friend of one of the great financial legends of our time, Benjamin Graham.

Graham, together with another Columbia University professor, David Dodd, first set forth value investing principles in their 778-page epic, *Security Analysis*. Although modified many times, the essential value investing concept remains unchanged: the shares of any sound company—even a boring, slow-growing business—are a fine investment if bought at a cheap enough price.

Graham was value investing's leading prophet, but he was more than that. He transformed investing from an art based mainly on Wall Street blather—imagination, guesswork, and inside information—into a methodical *discipline*. Graham believed that any conscientious investor could map a high trail through the slough of market fluctuations by paying close attention to investment fundamentals and by taking advantage of undervaluation and mispricing of individual securities.

Has value investing paid off? Yes, and I'll elaborate on and document that success in Chapter 1. In fact, value principles are justifying themselves even more thoroughly now than ever before.

Graham's philosophy was much akin to that of financier Bernard Baruch, who, writing of the 1929 stock market crash, said: "I have always thought that if . . . even in the very presence of dizzily spiraling stock prices, we had all continuously repeated *two and two still makes four,* much of the evil might have been averted."[5]

In other words: Fundamentals. Fundamentals. Fundamentals.

RECOGNIZED TODAY BY LIP SERVICE

Oddly enough, Wall Street respected Graham but never totally embraced his philosophy—paying lip service, instead. Informal, but very consistent, estimates are that no more than about 10 percent of the money invested in stocks is managed along value lines.

For many, value investing is too painstaking, too boring, and too disciplined. Few will stay the course since there is no excitement, no action in watching eggs that take years to come to a boil. Value investing strains too much the patience and will of the investor who needs courage to play against the crowd—often under trying circumstances.

THREE REASONS FOR THIS BOOK

This book is important for three reasons. The first is the need to remind investors that patience is necessary if big profits are to be made from investments. Put another way, it is often easier to tell *what* will happen to the price of a security than *when* it will happen.

The second is the need to redirect investor thinking. The stock market is inherently misleading. Doing what everybody else is doing can often be wrong.

Finally, American investors today have many financial alternatives that were not around—or effectually available—during Graham's time. It is important to address several of these issues as well in light of Graham's principles.

There is one group in particular I believe could benefit from this book—smaller investors with some experience in the market. In other words, *Value Investing Today* was not designed as a how-to book for complete novices or as a textbook, or for highly skilled professionals. It should prove valuable assistance, however, to small investors who've taken the first few steps. I've spoken with many of these people and have noted that some have picked up all sorts of investment ideas and notions that could prove expensive.

So, *Value Investing Today* addresses a philosophy and strategy that will help small investors be more successful. As you go through the book's pages, you'll discover sound methods of fact-gathering and interpretation and understand the need for discipline and patience.

Another point to consider. When I've talked with a group of small investors, the most striking feature has been the tendency for them to set sail on financial oceans without so much as a chart to guide them. In *Value Investing Today* you will find a way to draw up, adopt, and proceed with a conservative and effective investment philosophy and plan. It is a plan, I would emphasize, that has already proved to be a successful means of building wealth and conserving capital.

NOTES

1. Louis Lowenstein, *What's Wrong with Wall Street* (New York: Addison-Wesley Publishing, 1988), p. 1.
2. John Templeton, "Advertisement for Shearson Lehman Hutton," *New York Times Magazine,* October 23, 1988.
3. John Rothchild, *A Fool and His Money* (New York: Viking-Penguin, 1988).
4. Sereno S. Pratt, *The Work of Wall Street* (New York: Appleton, 1903).
5. Charles Mackay, *Extraordinary Popular Delusions and the Madness of Crowds* (New York: Crown Publishers, 1932), Foreword, p. xiv.

CHAPTER 1

REWARDS OF VALUE INVESTING

Sometimes investing seems easy. If you had purchased $10,000 worth of common shares of Xerox in 1960, your investment would have been worth $16.5 million in 1970. Suppose in 1982 you had put an extra $1,000 into shares of the Price Company. Cashing out in 1986 would have returned a heady $18,000.

That, of course, encapsulates the American dream: finding a "gee-whiz" stock that offers a spectacular run and a shortcut to wealth. Everyone has heard of someone who presently sails his new yacht off the coast of Mexico, thanks to the purchase of Genentech or Intel shares at just the right time. Unfortunately, such examples prove rare for most investors. For them the path, at best, has been full of gravel.

Even so, certain investors *are* obtaining superior results, watching their portfolios grow, taking some profits, and encountering minimal risk, year in, year out.

How? Not by listening to innumerable prophets, the ones that spring up during bad times with "new" strategies and advice. Nor by employing complicated theories such as market timing, efficient market, or asset allocation—in fact, any of the intricate tools of academicians or market technicians. (The IRS rarely receives estate tax windfalls from market technicians who have generated superior rates of return *over the long haul.*) And certainly not by happenchance or accident. These investors' goals are being accomplished instead by doing it the old-fashioned way—through value investing.

The purpose of this chapter is to review several rewards

open to the average value investor and the chapter begins by addressing four broadly defined benefits. Actual records of professional money managers, as well as results from performance studies, are presented.

The reader should keep in mind that value investing is not a get-rich-quick scheme or an investment panacea. Don't expect home runs. By carefully following its principles, however, prudent, rational investors may obtain four significant advantages.

FOUR BENEFITS OF VALUE INVESTING

The first benefit is that there is lower risk than is associated with investing through the use of pure growth or other strategies. Value investing is almost synonymous with capital preservation. Growth investors, for example, are subject to large permanent declines.

The second benefit is lower portfolio volatility. Even though a portfolio's *aggregate* value may fluctuate, the chapters ahead will demonstrate why that should not concern the average investor.

The third benefit is reduced trading costs. Since value proponents hold securities for extended periods it means, logically enough, buying and selling costs are cut. Profits go to the patient investor.

The fourth benefit is more pragmatic—the pot of gold. The bottom line is that value investing pays off in dollars and cents.

SEVERAL VALUE INVESTING YARDSTICKS

Seeing is believing. Consider the following two examples that involve Warren Buffett, considered by many to be America's premier investor and a value investor for most of his career. His credentials include generating annual returns in excess of 20 percent for Berkshire Hathaway shareholders in up and down markets for more than 20 years.

The first example involves a careful value-investing study Buffett compiled a few years ago.[1] For the study he used his own

EXHIBIT 1–1
Walter J. Schloss

Year	S&P Overall Gain Including Dividends (%)	WJS Ltd Partners Overall Gain per Year (%)	WJS Partnership Overall Gain per Year (%)
1956	7.5	5.1	6.8
1957	−10.5	− 4.7	− 4.7
1958	42.1	42.1	54.6
1959	12.7	17.5	23.3
1960	− 1.6	7.0	9.3
1961	26.4	21.6	28.8
1962	−10.2	8.3	11.1
1963	23.3	15.1	20.1
1964	16.5	17.1	22.8
1965	13.1	26.8	35.7
1966	−10.4	0.5	0.7
1967	26.8	25.8	34.4
1968	10.6	26.6	35.5
1969	− 7.5	− 9.0	− 9.0
1970	2.4	− 8.2	− 8.2
1971	14.9	25.5	28.3
1972	19.8	11.6	15.5
1973	−14.8	− 8.0	− 8.0
1974	−26.6	− 6.2	− 6.2
1975	36.9	42.7	52.2
1976	22.4	29.4	39.2
1977	− 8.6	25.8	34.4
1978	7.0	36.6	48.8
1979	17.6	29.8	39.7
1980	32.1	23.3	31.1
1981	− 6.7	18.4	24.5
1982	20.2	24.1	32.1
1983	22.8	38.4	51.2
1984 1st quarter	− 2.3	0.8	1.1
Standard & Poor's 28 ¼ year compounded gain			887.2%
WJS Limited Partners 28 ¼ year compounded gain			6,678.8%
WJS Partnership 28 ¼ year compounded gain			23,104.7%
Standard & Poor's 28 ¼ year annual compounded rate			8.4%
WJS Limited Partners 28 ¼ year annual compounded rate			16.1%
WJS Partnership 28 ¼ year annual compounded rate			21.3%

During the history of the Partnership it has owned over 800 issues and, at most times, has had at least 100 positions. Present assets under management approximate $45 million.

Source: Warren E. Buffett, "The Superinvestors of Graham-and-Doddsville," *Hermes*, Fall 1984, p. 6.

partnership records, those of three other fellow employees in the Graham-Newman Corporation between 1954 and 1956, and records of several other historic value investors. All of these value managers, year-in and year-out, have beaten the Standard & Poor's 500 Stock Index.

The first record (Exhibit 1–1), that of Walter Schloss, occurred over a 28-year period when he created a diversified portfolio that contained well over 100 stocks.

The second record, (Exhibit 1–2), was that of Tom Knapp

EXHIBIT 1–2
Tweedy, Browne Inc.

Period Ended (September 30)	Dow Jones* (%)	S&P 500* (%)	TBK Overall (%)	TBK Limited Partners (%)
1968 (9 mos.)	6.0	8.8	27.6	22.0
1969	− 9.5	− 6.2	12.7	10.0
1970	− 2.5	− 6.1	− 1.3	− 1.9
1971	20.7	20.4	20.9	16.1
1972	11.0	15.5	14.6	11.8
1973	2.9	1.0	8.3	7.5
1974	−31.8	−38.1	1.5	1.5
1975	36.9	37.8	28.8	22.0
1976	29.6	30.1	40.2	32.8
1977	− 9.9	− 4.0	23.4	18.7
1978	8.3	11.9	41.0	32.1
1979	7.9	12.7	25.5	20.5
1980	13.0	21.1	21.4	17.3
1981	− 3.3	− 2.7	14.4	11.6
1982	12.5	10.1	10.2	8.2
1983	44.5	44.3	35.0	28.2

Total Return 15 ¾ years	**191.8%**	**238.5%**	**1,661.2%**	**936.4%**

Standard & Poor's 15 ¾ year annual compounded rate	7.0%
TBK Limited Partners 15 ¾ year annual compounded rate	16.0%
TBK Overall 15 ¾ year annual compounded rate	20.0%

* Includes dividends paid for both Standard & Poor's 500 Composite Index and Dow Jones Industrial Average.

Source: Warren E. Buffett, "The Superinvestors of Graham-and-Doddsville," *Hermes*, Fall 1984, p. 7.

who, in 1968, helped form Tweedy, Browne Partners. Tweedy, Browne built its record through wide diversification. Occasionally, Tweedy, Browne bought control of a business; even so, the record of passive investments equals the record of control investments.

EXHIBIT 1–3
Buffett Partnership, Ltd.

Year	Overall Results from Dow (%)	Partnership Results (%)	Limited Partners' Results (%)
1957	− 8.4	10.4	9.3
1958	38.5	40.9	32.2
1959	20.0	25.9	20.9
1960	− 6.2	22.8	18.6
1961	22.4	45.9	35.9
1962	− 7.6	13.9	11.9
1963	20.6	38.7	30.5
1964	18.7	27.8	22.3
1965	14.2	47.2	36.9
1966	− 15.6	20.4	16.8
1967	19.0	35.9	28.4
1968	7.7	58.8	45.6
1969	− 11.6	6.8	6.6
On a cumulative or compounded basis, the results are:			
1957	− 8.4	10.4	9.3
1957-58	26.9	55.6	44.5
1957-59	52.3	95.9	74.7
1957-60	42.9	140.6	107.2
1957-61	74.9	251.0	181.6
1957-62	61.6	299.8	215.1
1957-63	94.9	454.5	311.2
1957-64	131.3	608.7	402.9
1957-65	164.1	943.2	588.5
1957-66	122.9	1156.0	704.2
1957-67	165.3	1606.9	932.6
1957-68	185.7	2610.6	1403.5
1957-69	152.6	2794.9	1502.7
Annual Compounded Rate	**7.4**	**29.5**	**23.8**

Source: Warren E. Buffett, "The Superinvestors of Graham-and-Doddsville," *Hermes*, Fall 1984, p. 7.

Exhibit 1–3 describes Buffett's own record. Those who initially placed $10,000 into Buffett's private investing partnership when it first opened in 1956 would have walked off in 1969, when the fund dissolved, with about $260,000.[2]

Exhibit 1–4 shows the record of the Sequoia Fund—a fund set up at Buffett's suggestion but managed by William Ruane. Total investment return for the Sequoia Fund through 1985 was 775 percent compared to 270 percent for Standard & Poor's. Sequoia Fund's average annual compound growth rate of 17

EXHIBIT 1–4
Sequoia Fund, Inc.

	Annual Percentage Change†	
Year	Sequoia Fund (%)	S&P 500 Index* (%)
1970 (from July 15)	12.1	20.6
1971	13.5	14.3
1972	3.7	18.9
1973	− 24.0	− 14.8
1974	− 15.7	− 26.4
1975	60.5	37.2
1976	72.3	23.6
1977	19.9	− 7.4
1978	23.9	6.4
1979	12.1	18.2
1980	12.6	32.3
1981	21.5	− 5.0
1982	31.2	21.4
1983	27.3	22.4
1984 (first quarter)	− 1.6	− 2.4
Entire Period	775.3%	270.0%
Compound Annual Return	17.2%	10.0%
Plus 1% Management Fee	1.0%	
Gross Investment Return	**18.2%**	**10.0%**

* Includes dividends (and capital gains distributions in the case of Sequoia Fund) treated as though reinvested.
† These figures differ slightly from the S&P figures in Table 1 because of a difference in calculation of reinvested dividends.

Source: Warren E. Buffett, "The Superinvestors of Graham-and-Doddsville," *Hermes*, Fall 1984, p. 8.

percent from inception through 1985 compares with 10 percent for S&P.

Exhibit 1–5 is the record of Charles Munger. Although a partner of Buffett, his portfolio differs from Buffett's, as well as the others, since value investors are independent individuals.

EXHIBIT 1–5
Charles Munger

Year	Mass. Inv. Trust (%)	Investors Stock (%)	Lehman (%)	Tri-Cont. (%)	Dow (%)	Over-all Partnership (%)	Limited Partners (%)
			Yearly Results (1)				
1962	−9.8	−13.4	−14.4	− 12.2	− 7.6	30.1	20.1
1963	20.0	16.5	23.8	20.3	20.6	71.7	47.8
1964	15.9	14.3	13.6	13.3	18.7	49.7	33.1
1965	10.2	9.8	19.0	10.7	14.2	8.4	6.0
1966	− 7.7	− 9.9	− 2.6	− 6.9	− 15.7	12.4	8.3
1967	20.0	22.8	28.0	25.4	19.0	56.2	37.5
1968	10.3	8.1	6.7	6.8	7.7	40.4	27.0
1969	− 4.8	− 7.9	− 1.9	0.1	− 11.6	28.3	21.3
1970	0.6	− 4.1	− 7.2	− 1.0	8.7	− 0.1	− 0.1
1971	9.0	16.8	26.6	22.4	9.8	25.4	20.6
1972	11.0	15.2	23.7	21.4	18.2	8.3	7.3
1973	−12.5	−17.6	−14.3	− 21.3	− 13.1	− 31.9	− 31.9
1974	−25.5	−25.6	−30.3	− 27.6	− 23.1	− 31.5	− 31.5
1975	32.9	33.3	30.8	35.4	44.4	73.2	73.2
			Compound Results (2)				
1962	− 9.8	−13.4	− 14.4	− 12.2	− 7.6	30.1	20.1
1962-3	8.2	0.9	6.0	5.6	11.5	123.4	77.5
1962-4	25.4	15.3	20.4	19.6	32.4	234.4	136.3
1962-5	38.2	26.6	43.3	32.4	51.2	262.5	150.5
1962-6	27.5	14.1	39.5	23.2	27.5	307.5	171.3
1962-7	53.0	40.1	78.5	54.5	51.8	536.5	273.0
1962-8	68.8	51.4	90.5	65.0	63.5	793.6	373.7
1962-9	60.7	39.4	86.9	65.2	44.5	1046.5	474.6
1962-70	61.7	33.7	73.4	63.5	57.1	1045.4	474.0
1962-71	76.3	56.2	119.5	100.1	72.5	1336.3	592.2
1962-72	95.7	79.9	171.5	142.9	103.9	1455.5	642.7
1962-73	71.2	48.2	132.7	91.2	77.2	959.3	405.8
1962-74	27.5	10.3	62.2	38.4	36.3	625.6	246.5
1962-75	69.4	47.0	112.2	87.4	96.8	1156.7	500.1
Average Annual Compounded Rate	**3.8**	**2.8**	**5.5**	**4.6**	**5.0**	**19.8**	**13.7**

Source: Warren E. Buffett, "The Superinvestors of Graham-and-Doddsville," *Hermes,* Fall 1984, p. 10.

EXHIBIT 1–6

Manager	Total Annual Return	No. of Years	Total Return in % vs. Average Stock (per year)	
Warren Buffett	23.8%	13	Warren Buffett	+16.4
Pacific Partners	23.6	19	Pacific Partners	+15.8
Stan Perlmeter	19.0	18	Stan Perlmeter	+12.0
Sequoia Fund	18.2	13¾	Tweedy, Browne	+ 9.0
Walter Schloss	16.1	28¼	Charles Munger	+ 8.7
Tweedy, Browne	16.0	15¾	Sequoia Fund	+ 8.2
Charles Munger	13.7	14	Walter Schloss	+ 7.7

Note: Results are not strictly comparable. The total periods differ, and the terminal dates range from 12/31/69 for one fund to 12/31/83 for most of them. Also, some use the Dow Jones, others the S&P Indices as benchmarks. Finally, *limited* partnership returns are used, which are after deducting incentive fees paid to the general partner. This understates the "pure" investment results, but the pre-incentive fee returns were not provided, and it is not believed that the major conclusions would be altered by such adjustments.

Source: V. Eugene Shahan, "Are Short-Term Performances and Value Investing Mutually Exclusive? The Hare and the Tortoise Revisited," *Hermes*, Spring 1986, pg. 26.

Skill—Not Luck

These records of value investors are simply chance results, a critic might argue. Then consider the performance time frame in Exhibit 1–6. Notice the data show annual returns, over various time periods, that would please most clients.

Were averages bettered each year? Look at Exhibit 1–7. Apart from Buffett's performance, the group generally underperformed for 30 to 40 percent of the years covered. Exhibit 1–8 shows the worst three consecutive years of performance for these expert managers. The percentage shown is the total of the three years versus the market average.

Interestingly enough, Buffett's study demonstrated that superior long-term records can occur despite miserable three- or even six-year segments. It also verified that short-term performance may well come at the expense of long-term results. The outstanding records noted above were compiled with apparent indifference to short-term performance.[3]

EXHIBIT 1–7

Manager	Underperformance Years	All Years Shown	Underperformance Years as % of All Years
Warren Buffett	1	13	7.7
Walter Schloss	8	28¼	28.3
Tweedy, Browne	5	15¾	31.7
Charles Munger	5	14	35.7
Sequoia Fund	5.5	13¾	40.0
Pacific Partners	8	19	42.1

Stan Perlmeter (Per year data incomplete, but underperformed in 3 of 10 years shown.)

Source: V. Eugene Shahan, "Are Short-Term Performance and Value Investing Mutually Exclusive? The Hare and the Tortoise Revisited," *Hermes*, Spring 1986, pg. 26.

LOOK AT TODAY'S RECORD

So what? a reader might say. Hasn't the market changed since 1969? What about institutional influence? a reader may wonder. What about the October 1987 meltdown? Good questions. Exhibit 1–9 indicates that stocks with low price/earnings (P/E) ratios—a common way to measure undervaluation—outperformed the S&P 500 in four of the past six years.[4]

Or, consider the following study, involving all NYSE stocks, that saw light in *Forbes* magazine and was conducted by Professors Michael Berry and Mitchell Stern of the University of Virginia's Darden Graduate Business School.[5] Berry and Stern found that $10,000 invested in low P/E stocks (the bottom 20 percent of the NYSE) at the beginning of 1962 would have been worth $754,167 at the end of 1987. If you had played the *total* market route your return would have been less than one third—$229,828. (Low P/Es are an element of value investing and will be discussed more in Chapter 4.)

The Virginia researchers also demonstrated that such stocks returned 16.8 percent annually compared with 9.9 percent for S&P 500 stocks.

What does that say? It simply says that low P/E stocks did

EXHIBIT 1–8

Manager	Worst 3 Years (in %) vs. Average
Pacific Partners	−49.1
Charles Munger	−38.1
Sequoia Fund	−25.2
Stan Perlmeter	−9.8
Sequoia Fund	−8.3
Walter Schloss	−8.2
Tweedy, Browne	−3.7

Source: V. Eugene Shahan, "Are Short-Term Performance and Value Investing Mutually Exclusive? The Hare and the Tortoise Revisited," *Hermes*, Spring 1986, pg. 26.

three times better over this prolonged time period. Naturally, selecting stocks with low P/E ratios doesn't always work. Add up the score, however, and the results are overwhelmingly good. Remember—nothing works successfully every year.

Other Professionals' Records Confirm

The records of others on the playing field of professional money managers also substantiate value investing. Over the past decade the author's value-investing firm has produced returns of more than 20 percent—compared to 13 percent for the S&P 500.[6] An oasis in a parched desert? Not at all. Note the records displayed in Exhibit 1–10 and compiled by Peter Cundill, a Canadian, and the late Max Heine as compared to the S&P 500.

Cundill has achieved a 21.7 percent annual return since 1977 in the publicly owned and audited Cundill Value Fund. Cundill and I swapped ideas in 1974, before this impressive record began, and discovered that even though both followed the value philosophy, we weren't clones. In fact—and this is important to note—*similar rewards were obtained even though few selections were the same.*

Mutual Shares, Short Hills, New Jersey, founded in 1949 by Max Heine and now headed by Michael Price, has kept to its

EXHIBIT 1–9
Time for Value Stocks

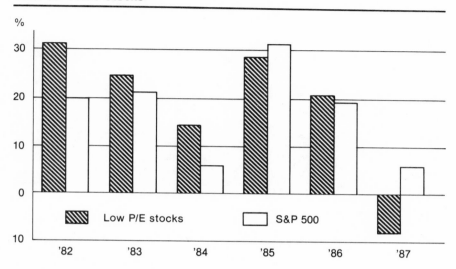

Although shares with low price/earnings ratios declined in 1987, they have outperformed Standard & Poor's 500 index in four of the past six years. Many analysts expect low P/E stocks and other undervalued issues to beat the market averages again in 1988 and 1989.

Source: Goldman Sachs, published in Marsha Meyer, "If You Can Steal It, Buy It," *Money*, March 1988, p. 129.

philosophy of "investing in securities that have a market value of less than their intrinsic value." Mutual focuses its attention on "special situations" such as liquidations and reorganizations. Recently, however, Price invested in Grossman's, a specialty retailer, paying $6 per share. He decided that Grossman's East Coast and West Coast properties made the company worth at least $10 to $12 a share.[7]

Can Such Stocks Be Found?

Efficient market theorists would probably answer resoundingly: "No. The market can't be beat. There are too many smart analysts that know too much about too many companies."

Well, maybe. Naturally, not every value situation turns

EXHIBIT 1–10

Year	Mutual Shares	Cundill Value Fund	S & P 500
1977	15.5%	21.0%	− 7.4%
1978	18.3	41.6	6.4
1979	42.8	30.1	18.2
1980	19.0	15.8	32.3
1981	8.6	18.8	− 5.0
1982	12.0	25.6	21.4
1983	36.7	44.1	22.4
1984	14.3	5.9	6.1
1985	26.3	22.4	31.6
1986	16.9	6.8	18.6
1987	6.5	12.9	5.1
Average	19.3%	21.7%	12.9%

out. But don't tell Schloss, or Cundill, or Buffett, or any other of the pros who currently take profitable advantage of specific value situations. Two cases in point that may be of interest: Gotaas-Larsen Shipping Corp., based in Bermuda, and Gulf & Western.

Gotaas-Larsen Shipping Corp.
Two value-investing colleagues picked up Gotaas-Larsen when it dropped from $12 to $4 a share as the result of worldwide shipping doldrums. The liquidation value of the shipper's fleet, which ranged from liquefied natural gas tankers to luxury cruise ships, was figured at $7 a share.

Last August, Gotaas-Larsen sold its cruise business, valued at $30 million in 1982, for $275 million.[8] Barclay Brothers, British financiers, recently offered $48 per share for Gotaas-Larsen.

Gulf & Western
Gulf & Western offers another value success story. At the end of 1982, G & W's book value was $28 per share. Yet, the stock was selling in the $15 range, or almost half of book value, after a year of lackluster earnings and several big write-offs had

produced a net loss. The dividend yield was a respectable 4.5 percent. Therefore, G & W's stock looked like it didn't have much downside risk, but had good upside potential if the company could get its act together.

In 1984 and 1985, G & W successfully undertook one of the most extensive transformations ever done by an American company. Investors quickly realized the restructuring was successful and G & W's stock sold for over double its book value by 1987.[9]

CAN ORDINARY INVESTORS USE VALUE INVESTING?

Granted, the examples above saw professionals involved. More relevant is the question: can ordinary investors successfully apply value methods? Here the answer is a resounding *yes*.

The charm of value investing—its mechanical simplicity—permits investors to utilize value strategies if they are willing to be patient, to dig, and to use a modicum of common sense. Far more fun and easier, but perhaps less profitable, would be wining and dining with advisers peddling great concepts. But rewards are definitely there. In Chapter 2 and the pages to follow, methods will be presented that will help turn seeming challenges and complexities into successful value-investing rewards.

NOTES

1. Warren E. Buffett, "The Superinvestors of Graham-and-Doddsville," *Hermes,* Fall 1984, p. 4.
2. John Train, *The Midas Touch* (New York: Harper & Row, 1987), p. 1.
3. V. Eugene Shahan, "Are Short-Term Performance and Value Investing Mutually Exclusive? The Hare and the Tortoise Revisited," *Hermes,* Spring 1986, pp. 26–30.
4. Marsha Meyer, "If You Can Steal It, Buy It," *Money,* March 1988. Source of chart, Goldman Sachs, p. 129.

5. David Dreman, "The Glories of Low-P/E Investing," *Forbes,* 1987.
6. Files, Brandes Investment Management.
7. Daniel P. Wiener, "Overlooked and Undervalued," *U.S. News & World Report,* September 12, 1988, p. 63.
8. Brett Duval Fromson, "A Low-Risk Path to Profits," *Fortune,* Fall 1988, p. 14.
9. Peter D. Heerwagen, *Investing for Total Return* (Chicago: Probus, 1988), p. 52.

CHAPTER 2

COMPLEXITIES OF VALUE INVESTING

"If the record of value investing clearly proves it's the road to Golconda, why isn't everyone scouring the stock pages for their own diamonds?" a skeptical telephone caller asks.

Good question. The reasons are not hard to find. The beginning of Chapter 2 presents a definition of value investing and then addresses several reasons why it's not everyone's cup of tea. The chapter also presents arguments on why the investor should "buy a business" and not "buy the stock" and why concentration on internal rather than external matters—the essence of Graham's particular time-tested strategy—can be profitable for investors. Chapter 2 also presents attitudes value investors have successfully adopted—including the "24-second" philosophy—as well as dispelling two current investing ideas that could prove harmful. Should you go against the crowd? The experts? Chapter 2 discusses why thumbing your nose at the experts could be the best step ever taken.

But, first things first. Let's briefly outline the value investing philosophy.

WHAT DO WE MEAN BY VALUE INVESTING?

Defining value investing can be chancy. Many investors claim to wear "value" hats. Such investors, however, have diluted the value recipe, shortened time horizons, or otherwise engaged in practices sure to make classic value investors wince.

The usual definition of value investing concentrates on

identifying companies whose shares trade at cheap prices, substantially below the companies' inherent worth. (Worth, in this context, takes into account a business's longer-term average earnings together with the price for which its assets could be sold.)

Benjamin Graham outlined two methods and strategies for evaluating stocks. The first was to determine a company's earning power, a strategy that does not fall within the scope of this book.[1] His second strategy, however, does fall within the book's scope.

Under Graham's second tactic, value investors essentially ferret out companies that trade for significantly less than book or net asset value. Other criteria also take part; I'll go into them later.[2]

The soul of value investing is to buy company shares at a discount. The heart is simply this: At any given time in the business world there are excellent businesses that attract a good deal of attention. Meanwhile, other segments are overlooked by investors. These wallflowers contain a wide variety of businesses where investments could be made—if the price were right.

That is a commonplace observation. What is not so commonplace, however, is this: While many businesses are not worth what they sell for in the stock market, some businesses are almost given away. These are the types of companies that cause a glint in the eyes of value investors. Or they should. The way to find them is by looking *internally*, that is, at the performance of the underlying business and also at its resources.

The average value investor pays no heed to *external* matters; that is, to the day-to-day market prices at which a company's securities trade, quarterly earnings projections, market volatility, price momentum, or volume. Comparative analysis plays a diminished role.

LOOKING AT A VALUE STOCK:
NATIONAL PRESTO

Graham cited National Presto as a typical value stock in the 1973 edition of his book, *The Intelligent Investor*. For his research on National Presto Graham used S&P statistics provided by the La Jolla, California, wire house where the author was employed. Since I was in at the beginning, I've taken the liberty of including the incident in this chapter.

At first glance, Presto was the kind of company a homemaker would love. The housewares maker invented not only the pressure cooker, but also the electric frying pan, the first steam iron that could use tap water, and the stainless steel percolater. The only thing it couldn't stir up was investor interest.

Even though the company's balance sheet was a thing of beauty, Presto's price had dipped to $21 in 1970 from a high of $45 recorded two years earlier. It was priced at four times earnings and 65 percent of book value and at a considerable discount from its net current assets of $27 per share. Earnings had grown from $0.77 per share in 1958 to $5.61 in 1968, when it was supplying shells for the Vietnam war. By March 1972, Presto's shares had risen to $34 per share and the company's shares were trading only at its enlarged net current assets per share and at 5.5 times earnings.

Graham was not loath to put his money where his pen was. Shortly after the new edition of *The Intelligent Investor* was published, Graham purchased 1,000 shares of National Presto at $33 per share. Interestingly enough, by March 1974, I'd formed my advisory firm and purchased Presto for my clients at $28.90 per share, including commission. It was then trading at a P/E of 4.5, net current assets were $41 per share, and the book value was $50. Cash items alone accounted for some $19 per share. Two years later I cleared out my shares of National Presto at $54.25 per share which was, roughly, its book value.

BUY THE BUSINESS—NOT THE STOCK

Investing in value equities should be treated somewhat like buying part ownership in a business—which, indeed, it is. In other words, it's the same mental framework.

Like any businessman, the value investor would aim to determine the company's *true* worth—that is, the company's assets and components—and what kind of wealth could be generated, that is, the *intrinsic* value of a business.

In the case of assets, the intrinsic value means what would be realized if liquidation occurred. In the case of earnings, it means the value realized by any excess returns expected compared to the returns of long-term AAA bonds.

The bottom line is simple. Value investors first, last, and always, figuratively, *buy the business, not the stock*. Essentially these two variables, price and business value, are all that should concern a value investor.

Lack of Mystique Borders on Heretical

It's easy to see that the above strategy violates almost all current notions of "proper" investment theory. The plain truth is that some of the brightest and the best professionals and academicians, who pontificate in grand terms of efficient markets, dynamic hedging, betas, and alphas, might find value-investing concepts too simple. After all, there's really no mystique.

Admittedly, value investing requires some effort. (Nobody said it would be *that* easy.) Then too, the application of several standards means that not every horse that comes by gets ridden.

Stock traders swear by short-term quotations. Market prices may serve if an investor needs instant performance and doesn't know much about the company in which he's investing other than a handful of statistics and the latest popular story.

Investors concerned about superior long-term performance approach things differently. To them, long-term performance means buying excellent values and then sticking with them. As a value investor you must look for mistakes in judgment or analysis rather than short-term market prices.

GETTING RID OF TWO MYTHS

One prominent reason why many investors shy from value investing relates to two Wall Street myths that are sold over and over. Perhaps a short explanation is in order. Although not strictly necessary in understanding "how to" invest for value, it is important for understanding value procedures. The first has to do with efficient markets; the second, with betas.

Efficient Market Theory

Many textbook-writing professors argue that the stock market acts efficiently. By that, they mean prices reflect everything known about a company's prospects as well as the state of the economy. Studying fundamentals is as useless and unreliable, so these pundits say, as reading tarot cards or tea leaves. The reason? Undervalued stocks, so it is claimed, simply don't exist. Smart security analysts have harvested all available information to ensure unfailingly appropriate prices.

Appropriately, our latter day storytellers have embellished their tales with jazzy computer printouts and a 20th century label—the efficient market theory. Like Gaul, their theory has been divided into three parts: **weak; semistrong;** and **strong.**

Efficient Market: Weak Form
Past prices have no bearing on future prices, so the weak form runs. Prices of common stocks are essentially independent; a *random* walk.

Generally, a value investor would have no quarrel with the weak form. Market or technical analysis of price behavior has never served adequately as a substitute for fundamental analysis. Tests have shown that a weak linkage between past and future prices does exist. Certainly not enough, however, to generate trading profits after paying the transaction costs.

Efficient Market: Semistrong Form
The semistrong form states that *all* public information has been incorporated into the market price. A changing mix of favorable and unfavorable information about companies, industries, the capital market, and the economy arrives fast and randomly at the marketplace. Broadly, that means prices behave equally haphazardly as information quickly translates into share prices. With rapid communication at our disposal, literally tons of information pour in.

Rapidity is not always the equivalent of accuracy. Rapidly transmitted information may draw one picture, however, a significantly different one may emerge when "slower ideas" are developed. Slower ideas may require interpretation and extrapolation.

Suppose, for example, an investor attends a trade show where he observes Company A has operational and deliverable widgets. Its competitor, Company B, has only a production model. Although neither widget has as yet been used, Company A will obviously realize more orders, sales, and earnings for the coming year even though those positive results won't show on the broad tape for some time. The slower ideas show Company A to be in a more favorable marketing position than was first evident.

Efficient Market: Strong Form

The strong form holds that security prices fully reflect *all knowable public and private information*.

No amount of analysis, in other words, enables investors to reach judgments that are different enough from the market price to earn greater returns. Indeed, efforts of security analysts to identify mispricings, plus the knowledge of insiders, create market efficiency.

Many value investors would argue the strong theory sounds nice on paper but that's about the limit. The reason? The strong form depends on the best of all possible worlds—where only logical, predictable behavior is exhibited. There is only one problem: The market won't play that game. The market simply isn't orderly or logical.

The "evidence" offered for market efficiency generally comes, in part, from a performance analysis of actively managed portfolios. In this respect mutual funds frequently become the guinea pigs. And, granted, different groups of funds do perform better than the odds say they should for extended periods. Perhaps the reason has not been chance, however, but disciplined security analysis with a logic both tested and validated.

National Valve Example

A good example of market illogic was the author's purchase of National Valve and Manufacturing Company (fabrication and installation of piping systems) for $13.75 per share. It sold at 2.4 times earnings, 2 times cash flow, with net current assets of $23 per share—including $19.35 per share in cash. The company had no debt. Therefore, cash and cash equivalent items were purchased at 60 percent of value and a 42 percent earnings yield was returned on the purchase price! Obviously, this wasn't an efficient and logical price. Later substantial appreciation confirmed the market's illogic.

Summary

Without question, most value investors would agree that market efficiency has increased through analytic techniques and recognition of sound principles. Careful study of market movements demonstrates several anomalies, however, including small company effect, the superior returns of low P/E ratio stocks, and similar phenomena. Those in themselves give the lie to efficient market theories. Finally, if all stocks have been efficiently priced, as maintained, the proven necessity for broad diversification would be eliminated. One would only need to match the right stocks with the right investors.

But that's not, nor ever will be, the case. Emotion and greed and inefficiency rule the market—not logic; not when stock prices can be influenced by the Wall Street crowd with prices set on the margin by the most emotional, greedy, or depressed person. In fact, market prices are frequently nonsensical.

This situation can be rewarding for the value investor, provided the gap between price and value caused by such inefficiency can be successfully exploited.

Beta Watch Out

The second Wall Street myth, the "modern portfolio theory," has cautioned investors to avoid high beta stocks.[3] Those stocks, in other words, that react extremely to market fluctuations.

The beta theory, of course, has absurdly oversimplified good investment practice. This has been pointed out by many, including author John Train. Train takes the beta theory to task in *The Midas Touch,* an excellent book that provides considerable insight into the current investing philosophy of Warren Buffett.[4]

Buffett, said Train, offered the example of being able to buy $1 worth of value in the market for 75 cents. Suppose the price declined so the same $1 worth of value could be had for 50 cents while at the same time the general market remained unchanged. Here, beta has increased but so has opportunity and safety. To reject opportunity because of an increasing beta would be absurd.

Parenthetically, you should forget about diverse notions such as capital asset pricing models or covariance, so beloved of modern portfolio theorists. Indeed, one supposes that most successful value investors would puzzle over their meaning and then concentrate on true concerns: price and value.

Consider Buffett's purchase of stock in the Washington Post Company 15 years ago when the company's market capitalization approximated $80 million. The whole company easily could have been marketed and sold for at least $400 million. (Their current value runs more than $2.4 billion.)

What if the Post's 1973 market capitalization had dropped even further—from $80 million to $40 million? Does that mean that real investors would have been frightened off by this adverse volatility? In other words, by the higher beta? Obviously not.[5] So much for the major myths.

VALUE INVESTING: AVOIDING THE PITFALLS

Now let's examine some of the challenges ahead. Don't be alarmed: They're not that hard. You don't have to be able to play three-dimensional chess. Successful value investing rests on carefully following the precepts and directions you'll find outlined in these pages as well as establishing a particular philosophy and temperament.

Philosophical Differences

To start right out, never concern yourself with predicting future developments. In contrast to growth stock investors who may live and die with projections, the value investor looks only to what is *indisputable* and *measurable* right *now*. (Obviously, certain assumptions are held: What is *value* in the past generally will be *value* in time to come.)

The average value investor has better things to do than scour financial pages for low beta, high alpha stocks. Little attention should be paid to "great concept" stocks or other popular wares a registered representative might peddle. On the other hand, as was noted earlier, the value investor must view value issues as if buying a private business. In some respects, value investors adopt the mindset of a *business* rather than a *market* analyst.

First, examine a company's economic value in relationship to its price. If you're satisfied, then appraise the people in charge—management. Perhaps the best way to accomplish this is by examining published operating results. Thus, as an investor, you have eliminated any emotional factors such as might come from a personal visit to the company. Factual matters can be double-checked by a call to a company president or chief financial officer. Failing to reach them, the investor can call the investor-relations department. A lot of these guys are like the Maytag repairman—lonesome. They love to talk.

No Room for Sentimentality
Here we find another cornerstone. Value stocks include every qualifying stock on which reliable data can be obtained. All are potential buys. No distinction rests between "big names" or "no names," personal likes and dislikes, or well-run and poorly run companies.

Poorly run companies? Think about it for a moment. Unexpected positive things will more than likely happen to companies where management is consistently incompetent or selfish. These could have a dramatic effect if the price is already low. For example, a sale or liquidation may speed up the realization of good gains for investors.

Keep the Right Attitude
Sometimes a grim determination to sit back and do nothing is the most important action for professional value investors. Many mistakes have been made by businessmen who were unable to sit quietly in one room and do nothing.

Patience admittedly goes against the grain. We've been

trained from childhood to "do something." Time and again businessmen have 'built up large cash positions and then have lost patience. The result? Cash has been plowed into high-priced acquisitions of misunderstood businesses—only for something to do.

Mobil Oil provides an excellent example. Faced with a large cash flow, management hustled out to acquire Montgomery Ward—much to management's later regrets.

On the other hand, Ford Motor Company, holding an extra $10 billion in cash, sits and waits. Perhaps Ford management can continue to resist foolish, high-priced acquisitions.

No 24-Second Clock in the Investment Business

In professional basketball either the player shoots within 24 seconds or the other team gets the ball. In the investment business you can dribble and pass the ball around until you get the shot you want.

The value investor should clearly understand the goal is not today's blue plate special—the hot stock of the hour, the stock with the most momentum. In fact, value stocks at first glance are never exciting or hot. It takes time before the value of a business becomes recognized—sometimes three to five years.

The goal of the value investor is not a sudden run-up and quick cash out, but finding an outstanding business at a sensible price, or a mediocre business at a bargain price.

Those bargain situations may happen for a variety of reasons. Perhaps the business has fallen from favor. Perhaps there's been a cyclical downturn or even short-term bad news. These events, and others like them, create the opportunity for which the skillful investor waits.

Cyclical Bad News

Again, take Ford as an example. In 1980 Ford sustained losses amounting to $12.83 per share. Ford's losses were due mainly to a simultaneous economic and car sales recession.

The result? In 1980 Ford's stock plunged to $18.50 and established a new low. More losses followed in 1981 and 1982 and Ford was temporarily on the ropes. That was indeed bad for

Ford Motor Company but it was indeed good for willing-to-be-patient value investors.

For the next three years Ford's shares fluctuated, dropping once as low as $16 ⅜. Currently, however, Ford's shares are being traded at the equivalent of $230 (before splits).

The point is value investors went profitless for the first three of eight years. But today they could cash in at 12 times over their original investment—not a bad return.

Short-Term Bad News
The effect of short-term bad news can best be illustrated by the recent gyrations that affected Union Carbide. Although the 1984 explosion in Bhopal, India, collapsed Union Carbide's share price, the eventual rebound provided the Bass Brothers with immense profits.

Going against the Crowd

Value investing has usually meant going against conventional wisdom. The average value investor will find it extremely profitable to simply ignore investment world chatter about what the market did and where it's going.

Far more profitable is to have the courage of your convictions. Whether the crowd agrees or disagrees remains unimportant. The plain truth is most people will miss the point of a value investor's decision.

For example, in 1987, many true Graham-and-Dodders, unable to find appropriate stocks, chose to hold Treasury bills while a bull market set record highs. That takes courage.

Obviously crowd-bucking is easier said than done. Most people contentedly follow, buying when others buy, selling when others sell.

Going against the Experts
Value investors frequently butt heads with experts. That's all right; it's not dangerous. The use of experts to pontificate and predict has a long tradition in Man's history. Commissions of experts have had an enviable record of telling us what happened

and why, but a lamentable score when they proceed from there to tell us what will happen next.

In 1486, King Ferdinand and Queen Isabella set up an expert committee, headed by Fray Hernanco de Talavera, to study Columbus's plan for reaching the Indies by sailing west. After four years' work, the committee reported that such a voyage was impossible because: (1) the Western Ocean was infinite and unnavigable; (2) if Columbus reached the Antipodes he could not get back; and (3) there were no Antipodes because the greater part of the globe was covered with water, as St. Augustine had said earlier. Fortunately, Columbus did not listen to the experts.[6]

Most people still believe so-called experts know more about the future than anybody else. Sometimes this belief becomes ludicrous.

That's especially true in market activities where investors have given blanket acceptance to recommendations without first thinking them through.

Experts Frequently Wrong

We are bombarded daily by opinions, free and otherwise. A week's worth of listening and/or viewing provides the average investor with the information that the market "was long in the tooth," "overstepped its bounds," or "climbed a wall of worry." The meaning of these phrases is left to the imagination. The same market activity is reported from differing slants then warmed up and rehashed for the evening news.

Would you profit by this counsel? Look at Exhibit 2–1, compiled from the recommendations made by approximately 75 leading advisory services for the 1971 to 1981 period. This exhibit shows that if they were correct, well, so are stopped clocks—at least twice a day.[7]

The bottom line is that most experts stand ready to get you in near the market top and out near the bottom.

Professionals Also Make Mistakes—Beauties

The weekly *Investors Intelligence* monitors 123 investment services. Its experience shows the largest percentage of advisers

EXHIBIT 2–1
How Investment Advisory Sentiment Trails the Market

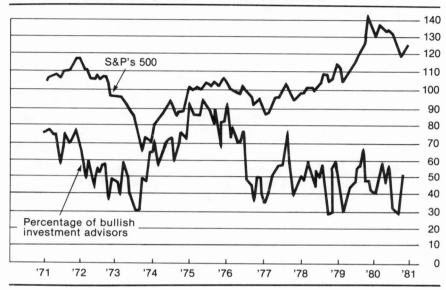

Source: *Forbes*, January 4, 1982, p. 298.

are bullish at the top—when prices are about to come down and vice versa.[8]

In short, most advisers, like their followers, have charged the wrong way at the wrong time. An investment record must hold up for a decade or more for any credibility. Moving with current "newspaper darlings" has always cost dearly. Yet many investors overlook that the law of averages dictates some darlings will have good short-term records and subjugate vital critical thinking. (Please understand the suggestion is not being made that good advice isn't available and that you shouldn't take it. Simply be careful to apply critical judgment to conclusions and recommendations.)

Three simple questions to ask yourself are:

1. Does the recommendation seem logical?
2. Can you think of factors that may have been left out?
3. Is what you're getting plain vanilla wisdom or a look behind the obvious?

Crowd-following traps professionals as well as novices. In fact, it helped me blow a decision concerning Union Carbide.

My firm had purchased Union Carbide originally in November 1981 at $48.50 per share. (For the sake of discussion the figures have been left unadjusted for splits.) Based upon value criteria, the purchase made sense. Union Carbide traded at five times earnings, 66 percent of book value with a dividend yield of 6.5 percent. The company's debt load was reasonable. Somewhat smugly I watched for three years while the stock appreciated.

Then came Bhopal. The public was inundated with scare headlines: Union Carbide would lose billions. Since the national debt seemed smaller than the apparent loss, I sold Union Carbide in December 1984 at 34 ⅛. To be perfectly fair, client pressures and tax considerations had also played a role. However, the wheel turned and things settled down. It became apparent that Union Carbide's losses would be much less than once anticipated.

Since then Union Carbide's stock has risen substantially— at one time topping $98 per share, when a takeover threat occurred. Consequently, selling Union Carbide at 34 ⅛ proved to be a poor decision.

CONCLUSION

Bear in mind that although the market knows what happened in the past, it cannot predict the future. Surprises make the market move.

Certainly, some elements can be estimated. We can assume that what has generally been true of business conditions in the past will continue to be true. Gross national product growth has averaged around 3 percent annually for 200 years and chances are it won't vary greatly. Profit margins have remained the same for the last 50 years. Usually the nature of a business does not dramatically change although no one knows how quickly the company's fortunes may shift, or, how a new product will sell.

In our next chapter, Chapter 3, I'll show you how to search for "businesses to own" and how to go about forming your value universe.

NOTES

1. Graham & Dodd, *Security Analysis* (New York: McGraw-Hill, 1934), p. 405.
2. Benjamin Graham, *The Intelligent Investor* (New York: Harper & Row, 1947), p. 53.
3. Beta-coefficient theories propose that securities prices are constantly and correctly assessing trade-offs between risk and reward. Low-quality securities appreciate and decline more than high-quality securities do. Beta itself is defined as a security's estimated market sensitivity. That sensitivity is measured in terms of an expected incremental percentage return associated with a 1 percent change in return of an index like the Standard & Poor's 500.
4. John Train, *The Midas Touch* (New York: Harper & Row, 1987), p. 55.
5. Ibid, p. 56.
6. Walter Wriston, *Risk & Other Four-Letter Words* (New York: Harper & Row, 1986), p. 54.
7. *Forbes*, January 4, 1982, p. 298.
8. Richard E. Band, *Contrary Investing* (New York: McGraw-Hill, 1985), p. 48.

CHAPTER 3

HOW TO FIND A
VALUE SECURITY AT
THE RIGHT PRICE

SCREENING FOR THE VALUE STOCK

So you've decided to become a value investor. What securities should you buy? *The Wall Street Journal,* the "Rosetta stone" of Wall Street, provides no clues. Open its stock-listing pages and a sea of companies swim before you in agate-sized type. So how does the value investor create a portfolio of value stocks?

Building a value portfolio is actually not all that hard. For the most part, only a few simple and logical procedures are involved. It's something akin to buying a house. Chances are when you house shop you're most interested in location and you screen out those that are unsuitable for one reason or another. In certain respects, that's how we build a list of potential value stocks. We do it by screening.

The present chapter addresses screening, point by point, and starts you on your way. Given that know-how, the average value investor can quickly assemble a universe of potential value stock candidates.

Don't worry if, at the beginning, the universe seems overly abundant. The two chapters to follow, Chapters 4 and 5, present practical tips and clues on how to whittle down the list to something manageable. You'll also be directed to spots where investment opportunities can be found offering a hefty profit potential plus adequate safety. How does a value investor build a solid portfolio? Where can the data necessary to evaluate value stocks be found? When should value stocks be sold? Answers to these questions are crucial to investment success.

Some Preliminary Housekeeping

But, first, let's do some preliminary housekeeping. Perspective may be heightened if four relevant points are kept uppermost.

Point one. Value stocks, simply put, are corporate shares that sell for less than the company's intrinsic worth. How much less depends upon the situation, but a good rule of thumb most successful value investors follow is about one third less.

Point two. Location or trading area is immaterial. Value companies are found in San Diego, California, or Amsterdam, the Netherlands. They could be listed on the NYSE or the Amex or over-the-counter. Excellent bargain stocks have been found buried among the koalas in Sydney, Australia, or mixed among the Volkswagens in Frankfurt, Germany.

Point three. The amount of sales or type of industry play irrelevant roles. Sales of value companies range all over the lot—from $5 million to $80 billion—and the companies come from any industry. (The average value investor pays scant attention to the copious lists of companies by sales, etc., published by *Fortune, Forbes,* and similar magazines.)

Point four. The final point rests more with psychological and analytical aspects but is exceptionally important: *invest only in what is understood.* Doing so means you won't give way to scare headlines that could influence you over the short term. Also, understanding the business acts as a spur and facilitates digging that may be necessary.

PUTTING TOGETHER A UNIVERSE

Identifying possible value investments sounds, and is, simple enough. Before starting, however, the value investor would find it prudent to broadly sieve out businesses to own from ones to avoid. Several suggestions on how this may be accomplished follow.

How to Spot a Business to Own

1. Look for a high return on invested capital over a period of years. That's always a good sign. The long-term average for businesses has been 12 percent to 13 percent annually on beginning capital.

2. Get a feeling for management—either in person or from published material like annual reports and so forth. We will deal later with "paper sources" but, for now, here's a worthwhile tip. Look for management that not only thinks like an owner but has staked out its own corporate share. That's a key clue. For example, if a president owns 20 percent or more of the shares outstanding then we both want the same thing—increased share price. Managers tied only by salary and benefits aren't rowing the same boat as shareholders.

3. Search for businesses that create profits in the form of real cash, not just generated by the magic wand of accounting. Earnings growth can be manipulated. This brings to mind an illuminating tale told by Abraham J. Briloff, a distinguished author and professor of accounting.

The story concerns an underwriter who, charged with finding an auditor, called in partners from several major accounting firms. Each partner was interviewed and asked, "What does 2 plus 2 equal?" Each of the respondents replied, "Four, of course"—each, that is, but the one selected. His answer, after some serious reflection, was, "What number did you have in mind?"

4. Check inventory turnover. Is it rapid compared with its industry? Is there a high return on the total of plant plus inventory? Are earnings predictable?

5. Glance over the company's business. Good businesses generally have defined products or services.

6. Look for managers who talk in terms of return to shareholders and controlling expenses rather than in sales growth.

The Noland Company, a Virginia-based distributor of electrical and plumbing supplies, serves as a case in point. Its return-on-assets and return to the shareholder over the years have been subpar. The company has for years continually communicated to shareholders in a manner that emphasized sales growth above all else. No mention is made that the sales growth has not been of direct benefit to the wealth of the shareholders. (In spite of that, the author purchased shares of the company when they traded below net net current assets per share and far below the market value of all assets and it turned out to be a satisfactory investment, mainly due to the low price paid.)

How to Spot Businesses to Avoid

How can an investor spot undesirable businesses? That's no problem either. In most instances, simply reverse the above characteristics.

1. Duck businesses loaded with debt. Mushrooming debt can frequently mean that things are going wrong. In that case, the company may some day collapse or have to refinance on unfavorable terms. A good rule of thumb to follow? *Businesses should have no more debt than equity*. Of course, that's not true in all cases. The rule doesn't apply to financial companies which live on the spread between borrowed money (deposits) and lending rates.

2. Run from corporate managers more concerned with perquisites, golden parachutes, bonuses—and excessively high salaries in relation to the return to shareholders. How does the value investor ascertain these factors? Simply thumb through a company's SEC-required data such as the 10-K report or notice of shareholders' meeting and proxy statement. This method might also be coupled with a quick glance at industry reports. They'll quickly provide going rates for top executives within that industry as well as other particulars.

3. Don't invest in businesses that generate money through accounting legerdemain rather than real cash. Such businesses also require more investment as sales grow. The result here, generally speaking, is a lack of working capital. A good method is to look at the cash-flow figures. A healthy cash flow indicates a company can pay all of its bills with enough left to buy shares, pay out a healthier dividend, or, invest.

4. Detour around companies that change character every time a bright new idea appears on the horizon. Many defense contractors, for example, promote vast, new, and risky programs just to stay in business. Other managers assume so much risk it is literally a "bet your company" circumstance.

5. Stay away from companies committed to providing services or commodities at fixed prices for a long time in the future. Inflationary rises could wreak havoc here.

6. Bypass capital-intensive companies. Many times the cash flow of such companies may not be enough to provide a satisfactory return and still maintain plant at competitive levels. These companies must fork up debt or equity funds regularly just to stay even.

7. Be particularly cautious about businesses subject to government regulation, such as utility companies. These generally don't make good long-term investments as their rates of return are limited by law.

8. Watch out for companies with different classes of stock. Here shareholders may be disenfranchised through limited or nonvoting stock.

9. Set aside companies with managements that only occasionally initiate cost reduction programs. Cost reduction should be ongoing.

One last tip: Keep in mind that the share price is an important determinant of the businesses to own or avoid. Companies with undesirable features could still prove to be good values if priced low enough.

How to Form Your Universe

Now that we know how to spot businesses to own and those to avoid, several yardsticks can be used in screening and narrowing down a value stock universe.

One key source for the average value investor is the *Standard & Poor's Stock Guide*. The *Guide* is really simple to use and has served me well as a primary data source for *domestic* value companies. The monthly publication covers some 5,000 publicly-owned companies. (Figure 3–1 illustrates two pages from this guide.) This material is quickly digested for each company.

Frequently, the *Guide* can help the value investor to decide right then and there to drop a company and move on. Perhaps the company violates one or more principles that have been discussed. The sooner the investor can make a decision, the sooner concentration can be directed toward better prospects.

Getting a *Guide* is a cinch. Most public libraries subscribe to it or a broker may provide one free of charge. Or, the investor can subscribe by writing the address provided at the end of this chapter.

The *Guide* is best suited for domestic issues, but worldwide candidates also should be examined. Although somewhat expensive, for *foreign* issues *Capital International Perspective* (CIP) proves quite useful. It contains information concerning some 1,750 foreign companies. CIP is published in Geneva by the Morgan Stanley group.

Both publications provide a barrage of information that covers a company's principal business, historic price range, recent prices, dividend yields, price/earnings ratios, and dividend history. Found also are basic balance sheet data such as cash and equivalents, current assets and liabilities, long-term debt, capitalization, and the last five years' earning history. CIP also includes book value, a figure neglected in the *Guide*.

OTHER AREAS TO EXAMINE

Consider also the following areas:

1. Examine particularly well the industries relegated to the old clothes heap by the public. For example, investigate banking institutions. Many remain under clouds and trade far below book value. That potentially makes them exceptional bargains.

2. Explore troubled geographical areas such as Texas.

3. Scrutinize companies hitting new lows in the stock price columns. The energetic investor will scour *The Wall Street Journal* daily in the search for value bargains. In most cases, it's

EXHIBIT 3–1
Standard & Poor's Stock Guide

142 Man-Max

Standard & Poor's Corporation

¶S&P 500 ●Options

Index	Ticker Symbol	Name of Issue (Call Price of Pfd. Stocks)	Market	Com. Rank. & Pfd. Rating	Par Val.	Inst.Hold Cos	Inst.Hold Shs. (000)	Principal Business	Price Range 1971-86 High	1971-86 Low	1987 High	1987 Low	1988 High	1988 Low	Aug. Sales in 100s	August, 1988 Last Sale Or Bid High	Low	Last	%Div. Yield	P-E Ratio
1	QMAN	Manville Corp	NY,B,C,M,P,Ph	D	2½	24	534	Bldg,construct,paper products	46⅛	1⅝	5⅜	1¾	3	1¾	10649	2⅛	1⅞	2	...	..
2	Pr	$5.40 cm Pfd([52]65.54:SF65)	NY	D	1	9	455	mining,fiber glass,roofing	64⅝	12	29	14½	26¾	17½	2945	26¾	22¼	25⅞	...	..
3●[1]	MDA	MAPCO, Inc	NY,B,M,P,Ph	B	1	157	15609	Coal,LP-gas pipeline:crude	62⅛	6 3/16	66⅝	39⅞	59	46⅜	8153	58¾	54¼	55¼	1.8	10
4	MAO	Marathon Office Supply	AS,P	D	30¢	4	38	Dstr office prod,furniture	9¾	⅛	3⅜	⅞	1½	⅛	....	....	....	....	...	..
5	MARC	M/A/R/C Inc	OTC	B—	1	37	1953	Mktg research,councel'g svcs	25¾	3	18½	8¼	17¼	12¼	941	16¾	15¼	15¼B	...	16
6	MAR	Marcade Group	NY,B	B—	10¢	13	1132	Apparel mfr:spec retailer	46⅞	⅛	7⅝	1⅝	4	2	1781	2⅝	2	2¼	...	17
7	MRCS	Marcus Corp	OTC	B+	1	28	1771	Restaurants:theatres:hotels	20	1	19	10½	16½	13	1900	15¾	14½	14½B	1.7	11
8	MRGX	Margaux Inc	OTC	NR	No	14	922	Bldg mgmt computer sys	17	2⅛	3½	1	3⅜	1⅛	3174	2⅛	1⅞	2B	...	d
9	MM PrA	Marine Midland Adj Rt[53]cm A Pfd	NY	NR	1	...	....		53⅞	40¾	52¾	49	50	43⅛	490	44¼	43⅛	42¼B	8.5	..
10	MARPS	Marine Petrol'm Tr[55]	OTC	NR	....	4	85	Oil & gas royalties-Gulf Oil	45	5	15¾	8¾	12½	8¾	168	10¼	10	10B	e14.5	3
11	MTLI	Marine Transport Ln	OTC	NR	10¢	19	534	Domestic,int'l shipping	11⅝	4½	10	5⅝	15⅜	7⅞	792	15⅜	14⅛	14⅜B	...	22
¶12●[1]	MKC	Marion Laboratories	NY,B,M,P	A	10¢	291	55625	Mktg ethical drugs:health pr	25	¾	41½	18⅝	27⅞	14⅝	62452	20	17	18¼	1.5	19
13	TUG	Maritrans Ptnrs L.P.	NY	NR	No	17	1358	U.S.coast marine transporter	....	....	9⅞	6	10⅛	7⅝	2843	10⅛	9½	9¾	11.8	..
14	IV	Mark IV Industries	NY,M	B	1¢	31	2253	Electr ind'l eqp:audio prod	17¾	1/16	19½	8⅞	13	9½	3691	12½	9½	10½	...	5
15	MTWN	Mark Twain Bancshrs	OTC	A	1¼	9	217	Comm'l bkg,Missouri,Illinois	23⅜	1⅞	22	17⅜	22	18¼	1528	20⅜	18¾	19¾B	3.6	11
16	MAKL	Markel Corp	OTC	NR	No	26	312	Insurance broker/underwriter	10	9	15⅛	9¼	17¾	13½	1173	16	14¾	15¾B	...	8
17	MFAC	Market Facts	OTC	B+	1	5	54	Mktg research & consulting	14¾	1¼	11	7	8	7	709	7½	7	7½B	4.3	16
18	MTY	Marlton Technologies	AS	B—	10¢	8	320	Computer phone support sys	29	2¾	5⅞	½	1⅜	⅝	509	1	⅝	⅝	...	d
19	MMPI	Marquest Medical Products	OTC	NR	No	19	792	Mfrs disposable medical prod	17	6¼	15¼	5	7¾	5	2028	7¾	5½	6B	1.2	d
¶20●[2]	MHS	Marriott Corp	NY,B,M,P,Ph	A+	1	303	40552	Hotels,food serv,restaurants	39	1⅛	43¾	24	33⅜	26¼	36883	28⅞	26¼	27	0.7	13
21	WMD	Mars Graphic Services	AS	NR	No	2	33	Direct mail mktg print svc	9	6	7½	2½	4	2⅝	248	4	2¾	2⅞	...	8
22	MSAM	Marsam Pharmaceuticals	OTC	NR	1¢	10	86	Dvlp stage:generic drugs	....	....	23¾	6½	16¾	8¼	1235	15½	13¾	14½B	...	d
¶23●[1]	MMC	Marsh & McLennan	NY,B,M,P	A	1	405	43245	Insur brokerage & agency serv	76¾	7⅝	72	43¾	58⅝	45¼	18821	55½	51⅝	53½	4.5	13
24	MARS	Marsh Supermarkets	OTC	A—	No	30	2483	Food chain, Indiana & Ohio	18⅛	1½	21½	12¼	21¾	15¼	469	20¼	19¼	19¼B	2.5	13
25	MRIS	Marshall & Ilsley	OTC	A+	2½	58	5499	Commercial bkg,Wisconsin	38¾	4⅛	33	24¼	30	27¼	1747	29½	28½	29B	3.3	8
26	MI	Marshall Indus	NY,M,P,Ph	B—	1	70	6682	Dstr electronic comp:tools	16⅞	½	25	9⅝	19	13½	3853	17¼	14⅝	15½	...	8
27	MRTN	Marten Transport	OTC	NR	1¢	14	809	Long haul refrig mtr carrier	20	12¾	23¾	5	7⅝	4¼	330	6½	5½	5½B	...	16
28	MLLE	Martin Lawrence Ltd	OTC	NR	1¢	19	1481	Publishes retails artworks	3¾	1½	8⅝	3⅛	9½	4	6667	9⅛	7⅜	8⅜B	...	13
¶29●[3]	ML	Martin Marietta	NY,B,C,M,P,Ph	A—	1	315	26207	Aerospace,constr'n mat'ls	48½	3¾	56½	35	48¼	38¼	22206	41¾	38¼	39	2.8	8
¶30●[4]	MAS	Masco Corp	NY,B,M,P	A	1	419	72160	Bldg & home improv't prod	34½	2⅜	40⅞	18¾	30⅜	22	60149	28½	23⅞	24¼	2.0	10
31 [4]	MASX	Masco Industries	OTC	NR	1	102	11043	Mfr oil field/ind'l prod	13⅞	1½	18¾	8⅞	14	9⅛	22118	14	11	11½B	...	19
32	MSCP	Massachusetts Computer	OTC	NR	1¢	43	5727	Computers for science/eng'g	16⅞	4⅜	13½	4⅝	7⅛	3½	21611	5⅛	4¼	4⅝B	...	d
33	MCI	MassMutual Corp Inv	NY,M	NR	1	17	331	Closed-end mgmt invest co	45	11¼	50⅜	34½	42	35½	521	38	35½	36	10.6	..
34	MSCO	MASSTOR Systems	OTC	C	No	30	3823	Mkts on-line data strge sys	30¼	1⅛	5¾	1¼	3⅜	1⅝	22040	2¾	2	2⅜B	...	24
35	MXC	MATEC Corp	AS	B—	5¢	7	280	Steel cable:electr:coatings	8⅞	⅝	7⅝	3¾	5¾	4¼	234	5⅜	4¾	5¼	...	23
36	MSC	Material Sciences	AS,M	NR	2¢	44	2626	Steel coil protective coat'gs	24⅜	8¾	28¾	10¾	20	11½	1988	18¼	15	15⅛	...	12
37	MTL	Materials Research	AS,B,P	C	1	20	1153	Sputtering, zone refining eq	39	⅝	10⅞	2¾	7⅞	3¼	939	7½	5¼	5¼	...	..
38	MAX	Matrix Corp[62]	AS,B,M,P,Ph	B+	1	33	2368	Imaging instrumentation	26⅝	⅛	19¼	3⅞	10	5½	8779	10	9⅝	10	...	d
39	MMII	Matrix Medica Inc	OTC,M,P	NR	2¢	2	10	Polymer prod & processes	84	3½	10	¾	1⅜	⅝	113	¾	⅝	⅝B	...	d
40	MC	Matsushita El Ind [64]ADR	NY,B,M,P,Ph	NR	[64]....	65	944	Japan mfr consumer elec eq	135½	6½	195¾	93¼	230	167¼	2830	230	187⅛	187½	0.3	28
¶41●[4]	MAT	Mattel, Inc	NY,B,M,P,Ph	C	1	94	18546	Major mfr of toys	52¼	4¾	15⅞	6⅜	9⅛	6⅛	18826	9⅛	8⅛	8¼	...	9
42	MW	Matthews & Wright Gr	AS,M	NR	10¢	6	232	Invest bank'g,municipals	12¾	8¾	13⅜	½	⅞	½	285	⅝	½	⅝	...	d
43	NUT	Mauna Loa Macadamia[68]	NY,M	NR	....	6	141	Owns macadamia nut orchards	10⅞	9¾	11½	7¼	10⅛	7¾	1327	10	8⅞	9⅞	11.1	14
44	MXXMC	Maxaxam Corp	OTC	NR	.001	4	330	Dvlp stage:Squirm Drive prod	11⅞	⅛	4¼	¼	¾	⅜	11837	½	⅜	⅜B	...	d
45	MAXC	Maxco Inc	OTC	B—	1	6	552	Auto prod/constr supplies	6⅜	⅜	3⅜	⅞	1¾	⅝	1326	1¾	1¼	1¼B	...	d
46	MAXIC	Maxicare Health Plans	OTC	NR	No	90	21498	Health maintenance programs	28½	7¾	18⅝	3⅛	4¼	⅝	46999	1½	⅝	⅝B	...	d

Uniform Footnote Explanations—See Page 1. Other: [1]P:Cycle 1. [2]Ph:Cycle 1. [3]Ph:Cycle 3. [4]ASE:Cycle 1. [51]Incl Chapt 11 liabs. [52]Thru 1-18-89,scale to $65 in '90. [53]Rate 7.20% thru 9-30-88:min 6%,max 12%. [54]Thru 3-31-93,then $50. [55]Units of int. [56]37 Wks,'87. [57]®$1.53,'88. [58]®$1.56,'87. [59]10 Mo Dec'85. [60]®$2.98,'87. [61]Fiscal Jun'86 & prior. [62]Agfa Gevaert Inc(11%)offer,$10 to Sep 1. [63]Fiscal Aug'85 & prior:12 Mo Jul'85 earned $0.80. [64]Each ADR equal 10 com yen 50 par. [65]®$6.60,'85. [66]Fiscal Nov'86&prior:4 mos Mar'87 earned $1.78. [67]Excl $62.5M subsid pfd. [68]L.P. Dep Unit Cl'A'. [69]100% non-taxable,'87. [70]37 Wk Dec,'86.

Common and Preferred Stocks

Splits		Dividends							Financial Position					Capitalization				Earnings $ Per Shr.								Interim Earnings					
		Latest Payment			Total $				Mil-$				Balance	Lg Trm		Sha. 000			Years											$ Per Shr.		Index
	Cash Divs. Ea.Yr. Since			Ex.	So Far	Ind.	Paid		Cash&	Curr.	Curr.	Sheet	Debt													Period		Last 12 Mos.				
Index		Per$	Date	Div.	1988	Rate	1987		Equiv.	Assets	Liab.	Date	Mil-$	Pfd.	Com.	End	1984	1985	1986	1987	1988							1988	1987	1988	Index
1		0.20	6-10-82			Nil			File bankruptcy Chapt 11				♦765.		4628 24001	Dc	2.18	d2.92	2.34	△5.79			6 Mo Jun		2.98	2.35	5.16			1
2		1.35	7-1-82	6-10			1.00		SF 5% ea Jan 19,'85						4628	Dc		3.60	b9.99	b1.46			Accum $32.40 to 7-1-88						2
3	1965	Q0.25	9-9-88	8-4	0.75	1.00			7.32	337	264	6-30-88	302		9928	Je	4.11	3.60	3.67	2.75	E5.50		6 Mo Jun	1.07		3.20	4.88			3
4			None Paid			Nil			File bankruptcy Chapt 11				2.80		1857	Je	□0.57	0.54	0.74	d0.74			9 Mo Mar	d0.53		d1.44	d1.65			4
5♦		0.088	10-26-84	10-9		Nil	1.00		6.40	212	537	6-30-88	0.86		3054	Mr	0.85	0.95	0.71	0.97			3 Mo Jun	0.21		0.21	0.97			5♦
6		A 0.10	6-15-72	5-24		Nil			1.23	91.9	42.2	4-30-88	7.41		1415	Ja	d2.33	d1.13	'0.13	P'0.12			3 Mo Apr	'0.04		'0.05	0.13			6
7		Q0.25	7-29-88	7-11	0.25	0.25	0.22		2.63	13.1	5.87	2-4-88	48.1	20	7672	My	'0.24	d1.04	d0.03	1.05	P1.31		9 Mo Mar	d0.13		0.01	1.31			7
8	1983		None Public			0.25			0.19	9.03	5.50*	6-30-88	0.21		6702	Dc	d0.24	d1.04	P0.18	P0.46							d0.04			8
9	1983	0.90	10-3-88	8-29	3.62¼	3.60	3.081			Callable at $51.50*				1917		Je	b1.05	b1.08	b1.12	b0.67										9
10	1966	0.356	9-28-88	8-25	1.065	1.45	3.217		0.86	1.30	0.01	3-31-88			2000	Je	2.38	2.03	1.15	3.15			9 Mo Mar	0.88		1.16	3.43			10
11	1957		None Since Public			Nil			Equity per shr $6.73			6-30-88	71.9		2930	Dc		1.00	d2.53	d0.64			6 Mo Jun	d0.29		1.00	0.65			11
12♦	1987	Q0.28†	10-20-88	9-14	0.28	0.28	0.17		57.7	269.	122.	3-31-88			150283	Je		0.23	0.35	0.61	P0.96		6 Mo Jun	d0.18		0.67	0.96			12♦
13		Q0.18¾	9-8-88	8-5	0.86¼	0.75	0.533		77.8	41.4	24.0		114		12250	Je							6 Mo May	0.40		0.70	2.01			13
14♦						Nil			204	402	81.0		435.		1061	Dc	0.45	0.68	1.20	*71.			6 Mo May	0.68		0.81	2.04			14♦
15♦	1970	Q0.18	8-4-88	7-25	0.50	0.72	0.60		Book Value $11.48			12-31-87	▢36.0	115	*7300	Dc	▲1.27	▲1.35	▲1.41	■*1.61			6 Mo Jun	0.68			1.74			15♦
16			None Since Public			Nil			Equity per shr $4.35			12-31-87	p20.8	57	*4250	Dc	◁0.57	0.27	◁1.52	◁1.65			6 Mo Jun	0.87		1.27	2.05			16
17♦	1954	Q0.08	8-12-88	8-4	0.24	0.32	0.32		2.24	15.2	12.5	6-30-88	0.17		1838	Dc	0.54	0.56	0.34	0.34			6 Mo Jun	0.12		0.12	0.46			17♦
18	1987	0.15	11-1-88	10-30		0.20	0.07		0.23	2.66	0.96	6-30-88			4358	Mr	0.55	0.38	d0.84	d0.90			6 Mo Mar	0.10		0.10	d0.60			18
19		0.05	10-17-88	9-26	0.20	0.20	0.16		42.0	928.	1176	6-17-88	2760		400	Mr	1.04	1.24	1.40	1.67	E2.00		24 Wk Jun	0.77		0.89	0.60 1.79			19
20♦	1978		None Since Public			Nil									116486															20♦
21			None Since Public			Nil			0.45	5.57	2.84	5-31-88	1.41		1618	Fb	p0.39	d0.50	d0.40	d0.46			3 Mo May	0.12		0.10	0.38			21
22			None Public			Nil			6.67	6.84	0.22	6-30-88			3320	Dc		▾d0.16	d0.29	0.46			6 Mo Jun	0.18		0.29	0.57			22
23♦	1923	Q0.60	8-15-88	7-5	1.80	2.40	2.15		298.	821.	521.	6-30-88			7200	Dc	0.81	1.04	3.30	4.96			12 Wk Jun	0.42		0.34	4.09			23♦
24	1960	Q0.09	8-15-88	7-6	0.45	0.48	0.41			Book Value $21.02		6-30-88	*49.6	185	p20358	Mr	2.34	2.23	3.00	4.53			12 Mo Jun	1.33		1.67	4.51			24
25♦	1938	Q0.24	9-14-88	8-25	0.69	0.96	0.83					5-31-88	p174			Dc	2.21	2.66	2.95	3.16			6 Mo Jun				3.50			25♦
26♦		5% Stk	3-25-82	2-19		Nil			0.95	157.	45.2	2-29-88	36.0		9097	My	1.54	0.78	0.39	0.69	P2.05		6 Mo Jun	0.37			2.05			26♦
27			None Since Public			Nil			3.76	13.2	2.76	6-30-88	20.6		3416	Dc	0.60	0.80	1.07	P0.71			6 Mo Jun	0.23		0.41	0.34			27
28♦			None Since Public			Nil			7.19	18.1	4.71	6-30-88	0.13		6632	Dc	d0.01	0.06	3.67	d0.48			9 Mo Jun	0.22		2.49	0.66			28♦
29♦	1954	Q0.27½	9-30-88	8-30	0.82½	1.10	1.05		157.	1174	1218	6-30-88	485		52905	Dc	▩3.88	4.36	1.56	4.65	E5.15		6 Mo Jun	1.73		1.93	1.93			29♦
30♦	1944	Q0.12	8-8-88	7-18	0.32	0.48	0.38		261.	928.	484.	6-30-88	921		137768	Dc	1.00	1.28			E2.40		12 Mo Jun							30♦
31♦			None Since Public			Nil			242.	788.	224.	6-30-88	1099		90050	Dc	p0.29	0.03	▢0.42	▢0.46	P0.53		6 Mo Jun	0.61		0.69	0.61			31♦
32	1972	Q0.95	8-18-88	7-25	2.85	3.80	3.65		16.7	14.0	13.5	12-31-87	13.2	9	14926	Je	◁0.42	0.02	▢0.11	'0.24	P6		6 Mo Jun	d0.53			d0.53			32
33			None Since Public			3.80				Net Asset Val $31.16		1-31-87	20.0		17208	Je	▩25.93	*28.29	*$34.42	$31.16										33
34		0.05	3-11-82	2-8		Nil			5.48	40.3	13.5	6-30-88	1.93		3148	Dc	d1.11	d0.61	d0.07	0.14			6 Mo Jun	0.03		0.13	0.00			34
35									1.02	10.5	3.5	4-3-88	2.82			Dc	0.41	d0.04	d0.04	0.09			6 Mo Jun	0.03		0.17	0.23			35
36♦			None Since Public			Nil			0.96	42.9	29.4	5-31-88	32.3		4955	Fb	2.00	2.10	▢0.20	▢d2.26	E0.90↓		3 Mo May	0.25		0.38	1.23			36♦
37		0.03	7-11-86	6-27		Nil			2.58	60.3	24.5	4-30-88	29.3		4153	Dc	0.93	0.63	▢2.02	▢1.66			3 Mo Jun	0.32		'0.19	d1.97			37
38♦		0.027½	12-30-70	11-24		Nil			26.7	110.	16.2	1-31-88	66.8		13003	Je	0.78	0.94	0.84	0.62			9 Mo Apr	0.35		d0.30	d0.64			38♦
39♦		0.315	7-18-88	3-24	0.315	0.64	0.836		0.14	0.93	0.79	3-31-88	2389		2484	Dc	d2.96	d2.40	d0.24	d0.18			9 Mo Mar	d0.43		d0.20	d0.52			39♦
40♦	1950		None Since Public			Nil			1228	22101	10278.	3-31-88			1861793	Mr	5.53	*6.70	6.50	6.73										40♦
41		0.07½	8-2-83	6-28		Nil			34.5	517.	292.	6-25-88	238.	67	47741	Dc	△*1.17	1.00	▢0.20	d2.26	E0.90↓		6 Mo Jun	0.01		0.07	d2.20			41
42	1986	0.27½†1	11-15-88	9-26	1.08¾	1.10*1.03%	1.03%			Equity per shr $4.05		12-31-87			6241	Dc	0.42	1.49	2.02	d1.66			9 Mo Mar	0.19		0.12	d1.97			42
43			None Since Public			Nil			0.03	4.54	2.35	3-31-88			4500	Dc			0.84	0.62			9 Mo Mar	0.08		0.15	0.69			43
44			None Paid			Nil			0.09	20.9	15.0	5-31-88	0.78	18	26690	Je	0.02	0.07	0.10	d0.18			9 Mo Mar	0.08		d0.06	d0.16			44
45			None Paid			Nil			0.03	0.09	0.55	3-31-88	17.0		4839	Je		0.56	0.02	0.54							d0.54			45
46♦			None Since Public			Nil			114.	339.	656.	3-31-88	293.		33787	Mr	0.43	0.75	0.13	7.65			6 Mo Jun	d0.64		d2.40	9.41			46♦

♦ **Stock Splits & Divs By Line Reference Index** ¹3-for-2,'84,'85. ¹³3-for-2,'87. ¹¹²2-for-1,'85,'86,'87. ¹¹³3-for-2,'85,'86,'87. ¹¹³3-for-2,'85,'86,'87. ²⁰⁵3-for-1,'86. ²³²2-for-1,'86.
²⁴3-for-2,'86.To split 3-for-2,ex Sep 13. ²³3-for-1,'86. ²⁴²3-for-1,'86. ²³³3-for-2,'85. ²³3-for-1,'86. ²⁴2-for-1,'85.2-for-1,'86,'87. ¹¹³3-for-1,'86,'87. ¹³3-for-1,'85.²4-for-1,'84,'85. ¹⁺¹-for-8 REVERSE,'87. ³³10%,'84 ²³3-for-2,'85.

Source: *Stock Guide* (New York: Standard & Poor's Corporation, 1988), pp. 142–43.

45

prudent to avoid big-capitalization or glamour stocks since everyone knows them. A good bet would be to look for companies that are registering one half of a previous 12-month high. Such a stock could well be added to an investigating list.

4. Study portfolios of value investors who have put together lengthy and outstanding track records. For example, study the mutual funds run by John Templeton to see if his stocks meet your criteria. Simply write for a copy of his shareholder's report; the stocks are listed in them.

Warning: Don't buy an issue just because some outstanding investor has done so. The investor must understand and have confidence in the logic of the purchase to avoid selling at the wrong time or for the wrong reason.

5. Scour financial publications such as *Barron's* or *The Wall Street Journal*. These publications print rosy things—and some not so rosy—about companies that Wall Street loves. Occasionally you'll also discover information about companies that meet value criteria such as having undervalued assets.

SOURCES OF FINANCIAL DATA

Here are some of the better sources of financial data.

1. *Media General Financial Weekly*

   Media General Financial Services
   P.O. Box C-32333
   Richmond, Virginia 23293
   Weekly; annual subscription $108
   In-depth statistical information on stocks and markets.

2. *Standard & Poor's Stock Guide*

   Standard & Poor's Corporation
   25 Broadway
   New York, New York 10004
   Monthly; Annual subscription $88
   Financial data, in compact form, on more than 5,300 common and preferred stocks.

3. *Value Line Investment Survey*

   Value Line, Inc.
   711 Third Avenue,
   New York, New York 10017
   Annual subscription $425
   One page reports and analysis for 1,700 companies.
   Industries updated weekly—all reports updated once
   every 13 weeks.

4. *Morgan Stanley Capital International Perspective*

   Morgan Stanley, Inc.
   1633 Broadway
   New York, New York 10019
   Quarterly: $2500
   Price and financial data on 1,750 foreign securities

5. *The Financial Times*

   The Financial Times
   14 East 60th Street
   New York, New York 10126
   Daily newspaper;
   Annual subscription: $300
   International news and prices

CONCLUSION

Chapter 3 has presented several guidelines about businesses to
investigate further and the ones to avoid. The screening process
was also addressed, as well as several key places to examine for
bargain issues. More filtering remains. The next three chapters
present more guidelines and tips for making your selections.

CHAPTER 4

THE FILTERING PROCESS

Several methods were presented in Chapter 3 which allow the investor to distinguish between "good" and "bad" companies. Even so, some "good" companies might be considered high risks; those we can do without. Chapter 4 presents four specifications that can be used as tools to analyze and eliminate "too-risky" companies. Addressed also in Chapter 4 are five tests the value investor can use to determine value as well as five tests for safety. Since one key factor in value investing is the margin of safety, the chapter defines exactly what is meant and presents guidelines for establishing one. Shortcuts to screening for value issues also have been presented that stick closely to Benjamin Graham's beliefs.

Eliminate companies if:

1. Losses were sustained within the past five years.
2. Total debt is greater than 100 percent of total tangible equity.
3. Share price is above book value.
4. Earnings yield is less than twice existing, long-term (20-year) AAA bond yields.

These guidelines are quite strict. Possibly the experienced value investor could ignore one or more but only if compelling and well-researched reasons exist. For example, an investor might relax number two if the debt has a low interest rate or if the company's earnings were especially strong and stable. Or, number three could be ignored provided the company has sustained high rates of return on book value. If that analysis proves too tricky, it may be safer to follow the guidelines.

FIVE TESTS FOR VALUE

Eliminating high risk companies will shrink the value list some; filtering for value will reduce it even more.

Graham listed five tests for value and five for safety. He did so not for professors and academicians but to rescue average investors who had become swamped by Wall Street's blather.

Stocks were true bargains, he believed, if they met only one of the value criteria listed below plus only one of the safety criteria.

The five tests for value are:

1. The earnings yield should be at least twice the AAA bond yield. (The careful reader will note we've already eliminated companies not meeting this criteria.)
2. The stock's price/earnings ratio should be less than 40 percent of its highest price/earnings ratio of the previous five years. (This simply quantifies the extent to which a stock has been knocked down.)
3. A stock's dividend yield should be at least two thirds of the AAA bond yield.
4. The stock's price should be no more than two thirds of the company's tangible book value per share.
5. The company should be selling in the market for no more than two thirds of its net current assets.

The five tests for safety are as follows:

1. A company should owe no more than it's worth: Total debt should not exceed book value. (In accounting terms, it should have a debt/equity ratio of less than 1.0.)
2. Current assets should be at least twice current liabilities.
3. Total debt should be less than twice net current assets.
4. Earnings growth should have been at least 7 percent per annum compounded over the previous decade.

5. As an indication of stability of earnings, there should have been no more than two annual earnings declines of 5 percent or more during the previous decade.

MARGIN OF SAFETY

One key thread that traces throughout Graham's work is the margin of safety. What did he mean by it?

Essentially, the scenario goes something like this. Although the future is unpredictable, we do know times occur when things don't go so well for businesses. When that happens the investor wants a degree of protection.

Purchasing a stock at a low enough price provides certain protection—even if future developments do not fare well. That's because the company's assets or long-term earnings power remain far above the firm's actual valuation.

Let's say investors purchased round lots of the shares of Company A at 50 percent of fair value and afterwards Company A fell into difficulties. Since the investors' purchase price was so low, even though Company A's value dropped, they still might come out with what was put into it.

Suppose on the other hand Company B's stock was purchased at 40 times earnings and traded at 5 times book value per share. Suppose also that serious difficulties occurred. In that case, the investor might never recoup.

I hope that scenario makes things clearer. The margin of safety provides a kind of hedge that takes miscalculations or bad luck into account. It is like going to the beach for a picnic. Chances are before you put down your basket you check the water line. You know that some waves will roll in more than others. So you put your basket down well back of the water line. That distance between where you place your picnic basket and where the waves stop is your margin of safety.

Shortcuts Speed Things Up

Human beings are constantly striving for ways to shorten things. It doesn't matter whether it's a new route for a trip to the store or a newer, faster office procedure, ways are devised to do it quicker and better.

That holds true in value investing as well. So the prudent investor could benefit from two shortcuts. Both save considerable time and energy. The first deals with P/E multiples. The second shortcut takes into account a company's net net value.

Track P/E Multiples

Tracking P/E multiples works superbly for at least the first fast run-through. As a value investor, you simply flip open the *Standard & Poor's Stock Guide* and hunt for companies with P/E multiples lower than six times earnings, based on current interest rate levels. (Incidentally, the P/E ratio is the current price of the stock divided by the annual earnings per share.)

For example, suppose XYZ company's stock sells for $10 a share. Suppose, also, that XYZ earns $1 per share in a year. Then XYZ's P/E ratio for that year is the $10 stock price divided by the $1 of earnings, or 10.

The hunt's not all that hard. Simply track down each page until a candidate's been spotted. Then cross out those listed above until the last targeted hopeful has been reached. Any stocks that meet the above P/E goal qualify as potential bargains. The more a company earns relative to its stock price the lower its P/E. It follows then, the lower the P/E the better the bargain. Comparing P/E ratios of similar stocks helps determine the best buy.

(The entire stock market has an overall P/E—a good indication of the current level of the market. The S&P 500 Index currently registers 12.7. Optimistic investors (bulls) bid up P/Es as higher prices are paid for shares. With pessimistic investors (bears), P/Es fall so low that many stocks are bargains.)

The Net Net Method

Examining the net net current assets of a company can also be a very effective screening process. Here's how to put it into practice.

Again, the value investor can flip open a *Standard & Poor's Stock Guide* and locate a candidate company. The next step would be to subtract the company's *current liabilities* from its *current assets*. (They are listed under "Financial Condition".) From that number subtract the company's *long-term debt*.

Divide that number by the number of *shares outstanding*. That presents the net net current assets per share.

Compare the net net current assets per share to the *stock price*. (This is found on the facing page.) If the price turns out to be one third less, a qualifying company has been found.

It really isn't as terribly complicated and confusing as it may seem. Screening, at the most, takes only a few hours—only a good morning's work. Compact discs are available with data bases that can prove highly beneficial for source material.

Shortcuts Follow Graham's Path

Shortcuts are only shortcuts, however. No magic wand eliminates homework.

Graham's most famous theory, as described above, was that investors should buy stocks at prices of no more than two thirds of the company's current assets (cash and equivalents on hand including immediately salable inventory), minus all liabilities (including off balance sheet liabilities such as capital leases or unfunded pension liabilities). Nothing was paid for permanent assets such as property, plant, equipment, or intangible assets such as goodwill.

Graham also held that if a company traded at two thirds of net net current assets and was profitable, then investors needed no other yardstick.

"What about companies that qualified except for current losses?" I asked Graham. Those companies, he believed, were dangerously situated. Losses constantly burn up corporate assets and could incinerate the appropriate margin of safety.

GRAHAM'S SECOND BEST-KNOWN METHOD

Graham's other dictum, slightly more complicated, involved three linked parts: earnings yield, dividend yield, and balance sheet debt.

Earnings Yield

Bargain stocks, he believed, required earnings yields of more than twice those of triple-A long-term bonds. (Yield is just another way of saying rate of return on your investment.)

So what is meant by *earnings yield?* Here is an example.

Suppose Black Company's security sells at 10 times earnings. That means it has a 10 percent earnings yield. Suppose White Company's security sells at five times earnings. Here the yield is 20 percent. In other words, the earnings yield is the reciprocal of the P/E ratio.

(Caution: Don't confuse earnings yield with dividend yield. Both yields are expressed as a percentage of the market price but the dividend yield is the amount actually paid shareholders.)

Suppose triple-A bonds yield 8 percent. Then examine stocks that have earnings yields of 16 percent or better. In other words, the value investor would investigate stocks that sell for no more than six and a quarter times earnings.

Suppose triple-A bonds instead yield 7 percent. Then, to be an appropriate value stock, the earnings yield would need to be 14 percent—the same as seven times earnings.

Clearly, if interest rates are low, stock purchases can be made at higher P/E ratios. This is just a commonsense observation. Most investors compare dividend yields or total return from stocks with yields derived from various types of bonds.

Dividend Yield

Dividend yield was the next segment of Graham's tri-part criteria. Dividend yields, he said, must be no less than two thirds of triple-A bond yields. In other words, when bonds yield 9 percent, the value investor looks for stock dividend yields of no less than 6 percent.

Balance Sheet Debt

Balance sheet debt was Graham's final leg. His general rule here was companies shouldn't carry more debt than they're worth. Graham reasoned debt created heavy interest expense that could easily drain a company. Companies can stumble and fall. That's why we cautioned earlier about companies that carried a lot of debt. Investing in those companies means you're gambling on future earnings being high enough to comfortably pay it. Better to scout out companies with small debt loads.

In 1984, triple-A bond yields approximated 12 percent. Using the approach that has been outlined above, an investor would seek out companies where the earnings yielded 24 percent, the P/E approximated 4.2 or lower, and the dividend yield was 8 percent or higher. A tough test to meet, to be sure, but not impossible.

Examples of Graham's Second Best-Known Method

During 1984, ITT Corp., the largest U.S. conglomerate, had sold at a low of $20 per share. At that price, the company's P/E was 4.5 times the previous year's earnings and the dividend yield was 9 percent. Total debt for ITT approximated $3 billion and net worth was $6 billion. Readers will quickly see that ITT, at $20.50, met value criteria, given a slight leeway on the P/E ratio. They would be right. Within two years ITT's stock price had advanced to $59.50.

The value investor should understand that, in periods of high interest rates, these criteria could be difficult to meet. Perhaps if interest rates were clearly headed down they could be somewhat relaxed. For instance, the P/E and yield criteria could be reduced a point or two, although I would not recommend relaxing the balance sheet debt requirement.

A second example demonstrates the reasoning. In 1987, to set the stage, triple-A bonds yielded approximately 9 percent which, of course, dictated a P/E ratio below 6 and a dividend yield of at least 6 percent.

A Norwegian building materials company, Aker Norcem, was selling at 50 Kroner per share; at 4.4 times earnings; with a dividend yield of 6.5 percent. But the company's debt was four times the net worth; only 19 percent of the company's capitalization was in common equity. As a result, Aker Norcem did not meet the criteria for balance sheet strength. At the end of 1988, the share price of Aker Norcem had dropped to 48 Kroner.

HOW SMALL IS A SMALL DEBT LOAD?

How small is small? The investor should look for debt payments that are no more than one third of a company's earnings at their cyclical low. That's a good rule of thumb although it isn't hard and fast; the debt level depends upon the nature of the company and its business.

For example, firms such as equipment leasing companies live and die by debt financing. Chances are such companies carry more debt than oil exploration and development firms. Financial companies such as banks use borrowed funds that, for the main, originate from customers' savings and checking accounts. Their profit comes from the spread—the difference between the cost of the borrowed money and what can be achieved with it. Solidly financed banks may have only 6 percent of total assets in equity and the rest mainly borrowed. Surprisingly, that could be considered a safe balance sheet.

In general, utilities pile up more obligations than industrial companies since they're guaranteed a certain return.

Now let's begin the fine tuning. The focus will be narrowed somewhat more in Chapter 5.

CHAPTER 5

NARROWING YOUR FOCUS

Now the real work begins: the hard-headed and pragmatic analysis of a company. One basic rule of investing is to "get the facts before you invest."

"The facts" in the case of value investors would include a company's history and type of business as well as its potential for cyclical highs and lows. Storing away facts may seem boring, but if facts are kept, carefully examined, and then used correctly, the investor stands a far greater chance for success.

It has been said value investors in many ways resemble detectives and there is a good deal of merit in that. By that is meant the investor should obtain all information possible—but instead of taking it at face value, should think it through.

Chapter 5 presents the type of information available—the paper trail. Included also are tips and clues regarding what the investor should look for and of what to be wary. At first, much of the reading material will seem like hopeless jargon. Don't be discouraged. It's like anything else. The necessary insight will develop after reading a few of the documents.

DIG! DIG! DIG!

Consider Jim Kennedy, a young securities analyst for T. Rowe Price, who once traveled to the South African gold fields to seek first-hand information about gold stocks.

In South Africa, Kennedy journeyed two miles underground to explore one of the world's deepest mines. His quest then took

Kennedy to the far north of Canada where a new generation of gold-mining companies had emerged.[1]

The lengths Kennedy went to aren't necessary for everyone. Certainly not for the average investor. But the investor does need to scan financial and narrative material prepared by companies along SEC guidelines. Chances are some real gems will be discovered.

FOOD FOR THOUGHT—AND INVESTING

Following are the documents that should receive special attention:[2]

- **Form 10-K** is the official *annual* business and financial report most companies must file with the SEC.
- **Form 10-Q** is the *quarterly* financial report. Included are material and extraordinary events that occurred during the reported three-month period.
- **Form 8-K** is a report to the SEC *within 15 days* of unscheduled material events or corporate changes.
- **Annual reports to shareholders** are the most important way most public corporations communicate directly with shareholders.
- **Quarterly reports to shareholders** are statements many companies mail directly to their shareholders.
- **Notice of annual meeting and proxy statements** are mailed to shareholders to solicit votes for election of directors and to disclose matters including officer salaries and insider and significant stock holdings. Companies not soliciting proxies disclose such information in Part II of Form 10-K.
- **Merger proxy statements** are issued when shareholders are to vote on an asset—conversion matter. That could run from a merger or consolidation sale of assets to a liquidation. Sometimes, when new securities are to be issued, the merger proxy statement does double duty. It serves as a prospectus and also is registered as an S-14 Registration.

- **Prospectuses** are part of registration statements and are issued when securities are to be offered publicly. The principal registration forms are the S-1 (a generalized form) and the S-7, a short form used by companies with relatively healthy operating histories.
- **Cash tender offering circulars** are made available to shareholders when a publicly announced offer is made to buy shares for cash from a general list of shareholders.

TWO REASONS MATERIAL IS USEFUL

Once the information has been gathered, how useful is it? How limited? In contrast to "smart-money" traders, value investors would find such data useful for at least two reasons.

The first is that the information is straightforward and trustworthy. Few liars exist among those responsible for preparing the documents, if only for one pragmatic reason—few professionals, lawyers, accountants, or investment bankers, are going to jeopardize their livelihoods and/or reputations for the benefit of management and large shareholders. (That isn't to say the documents are wholly complete and accurate. Most of the shortcutting tends to center around relative judgments as to what is material and hence should be disclosed.)

Second, document preparation follows two well-established rules. The first is to follow the specific form. The second is to look out for antifraud provisions. The latter provision makes it unlawful, in connection with the purchase or sale of any security for any person, directly or indirectly, "to make any untrue statement of a material fact or to omit to state a material fact. . . ."

Naturally, all documents aren't perfect. Nothing ever is. And, certainly, documents will not tell the investor everything the investor needs to know. But the paper trail provides an excellent way to avoid securities that would be unattractive at any price.

Pay close attention to the auditors' letter, found at the end of a company's audited financial statements. Such letters can be "clean"—presented without qualification—two paragraph affairs. If, however, the letters are "subject to" certain conditions, the investor should view them with special scrutiny. Study the audited financial statements, including footnotes. Chances are some potential corporate obligations have been buried there.

The investor should clearly understand that other factors might go undisclosed. For example, a business may enjoy a strong financial position only because it fails to modernize or replace outdated facilities. In that case, the strong balance sheet will dissipate in future years as the business suffers operating losses, embarks on massive capital-expenditure programs, or both.

Look in the proxy statement disclosures for clues regarding the overreaching of management. Here the investor can examine management compensation, insider borrowing, and certain sweetheart transactions between management and the corporation it serves. Form 10-K and financial statement footnote disclosures about litigation provide potential security holders with knowledge concerning potential losses.

OTHER CLUES TO BE FOUND

What else? Clues abound regarding future earnings, large cash distributions, whether the company is a takeover candidate, or whether it could be profitably liquidated or recapitalized in whole or part. The business descriptions found in disclosure materials prove helpful to investors in understanding an enterprise.

As stated before, the paper trail enables a value investor to pinpoint companies to *run from*. It might be a company whose financial position is so bad the entire business belongs to creditors. It could be a firm where management's prime goal is milking the firm.

Watch for Shortcomings

The investor should understand that the paper trail doesn't provide total information. Unfortunately there is no way for the average investor to look into the future or learn a corporation's innermost secrets. For value investors, however, that particular drawback promises less serious consequences than for investors who follow other avenues.

The paper trail is the obvious starting point and will provide most of the information the investor will need.[3]

How to Get Documents

The easiest way to obtain shareholder material and SEC documents is to write the issuer. In most instances, companies are happy to provide such information. Another way to obtain such information is to write the Securities & Exchange Commission. The SEC has copies of materials filed on microfiche cards in its main office in Washington and (except for Schedules 13D and 14D) in its regional offices. These are made available to the public in public reference rooms. Professional services, for a fee, will acquire and mail materials.

Be Wary of What You Read

Keep in mind that annual reports are really company sales documents. So look closely for what is measurable and not someone's opinion.

Most readers see the printed word as gospel and remain content to let others analyze and interpret. Doing this can be dangerous—with annual reports as well as the mass media. The media has always dispensed a mixture of fact and opinion or interpretation. Try to sift and separate fact from opinion, especially in financial news. The fact that the *New York Times* claims a person is an authority doesn't make it so or even make compelling his opinions about future events.

Read widely and critically. This helps you to develop your own particular viewpoint. Pay special attention to books and periodicals taking an untrammeled approach to investing and human nature. Even though *Value Line* and similar publications can be of great assistance, the value investor should think independently.

Reports have their own biases, too, and investors must understand them. For example, *Value Line's* ranking system includes *momentum* in with basic value analysis. Value investors ignore momentum and will have to adjust for this factor.

Digging up your own fundamental information permits you to make your mind up based on your own value criteria. You know your assumptions; you're aware of each bias. This can be vital in making buy and sell decisions.

NOTES

1. *The Price Report,* T. Rowe Price Newsletter, Fall 1987, p. 6.
2. Much of the following material was obtained from Disclosure, a worldwide firm that provides facts about public companies that trade their securities on the NYSE, AMEX, or over-the-counter. Disclosure's main address and phone number are:
   Disclosure
   5161 River Road
   Bethesda, MD 20816
   (301) 951–1300
3. More extensive treatment of the preceding material can be found in Martin J. Whitman and Martin Shubik, *The Aggressive Conservative Investor* (New York: Random House, 1979).

CHAPTER 6

FINANCIAL STATEMENT ANALYSIS

The basic aim of this book is to show the average investor how to build wealth by investing in public companies. To do that, more foundation must be laid; after all, no builder starts with the roof.

BASIC FINANCIAL ACCOUNTING

That's why it's important to know something about basic financial accounting. The importance of understanding financial accounting cannot be overestimated by value investors. In fact, financial accounting is the single most important analytical tool the investor can use.

That's because accounting is the cornerstone of disclosure in connection with each and every business. Whether a multi-million-dollar corporation or a single individual is involved, the investor cannot determine where the truth lies without some knowledge of accounting. The investor must be able to notice changes in the accounting system of a company and be able to interpret the significance of that change. For instance, why has management switched from LIFO to FIFO (two means of valuing inventory)? Other questions emerge from a careful study of the figures.

An investor without a knowledge of accounting would be at a considerable disadvantage. There may be some skillful investors who are baffled by accounting—but not many.

The suggestion is not being made to spend four years studying accounting. Most of us don't have the time, or the inclination. Let me provide the good news. Although financial statement analysis can become highly complicated, all the math needed has already been learned—in junior high.

Why? Because only a few simple tests are necessary to determine whether or not a stock is worthwhile. To make it easier, several major brokerage firms now publish pamphlets that demonstrate how to perform these tests.

The three major financial statements to study are the balance sheet, the income statement, and the statement of cash flows. The balance sheet is the financial statement that shows the nature and the amounts of a business's assets, liabilities, and stockholders' equity, as of a certain date.

My personal experience dictates that the areas to be examined by an investor should include asset values, debt, and the nature of the debt. That is, when the debt is due, interest rate to be paid, and the ratio of debt to equity.

Next, explore a firm's corporate equity. What is its *true* value? Is it worth more or less than stated? Perhaps the company has antiquated plants or outdated inventory. Perhaps the company has a binful of goods worth less on sale than they cost to manufacture. In other words, the investor should look behind the figures to the reality. That's the only way to compute true intrinsic value of a company.

Always keep in mind the story related earlier: "How much is 2 and 2?" Ask if the numbers are "real." Even though financial statements must be prepared according to generally accepted accounting principles (GAAP), these practices vary widely. One firm might write off assets faster than another.

Examine Inventory

Take inventory, for example. Company A might value inventory by using a method called LIFO, which means "Last-in, first-out", while Company B might use a method called FIFO, or "First-in, first-out." The inventory method drastically affects reported earnings, especially during inflationary times, and should be taken into account.

Case of Handy and Harman

Here is a good example. Handy and Harman, a fabricator and refiner of precious metals, including gold and silver, reported earnings of 55 cents per share in 1987.

It happened that the market price of gold and silver went up during 1987. In turn, that meant the real value of Handy and Harman's inventory also increased by $51 million or $3.67 per share pretax. Instead of using FIFO to value its inventory—which would have included the $51 million increase—Handy and Harman employed LIFO. That kept the valuation the same.

The value investor isn't interested in the concept of what is proper or fair under generally accepted accounting principles. The real issue to be addressed is what happened—not what the methodology said happened. As the reader can see, large differences can exist between reported earnings figures depending on whether FIFO or LIFO are used.

Watch Out for "Managed" Earnings

The income statement shows a business's earnings over a period of time and perhaps a word should be inserted about corporate gamesmanship with the income statement.

For example, given a downturn in earnings, management may try to boost them by selling assets. Such a sale—a piece of property or a building—is a one-time, or extraordinary, sale and may not occur again. Profits from selling assets should not be considered as part of the basic earning power of a company. The investor should subtract that type of sale when basic earnings are determined.

For example, Sea Containers, Ltd. received $200 million from the sale of an office complex during the first quarter of 1987. This can hardly be considered part of basic long-term earnings power.

Perhaps earnings were strong. In this instance, management may write off obsolete equipment or sell assets at a loss either to smooth earnings or for a tax savings. In both cases, the true basic earnings have been distorted. The investor must dig beneath the surface to get the facts.

SAVINGS AND LOAN ASSOCIATIONS

Bottom-line earnings from savings and loan associations can be misleading. Income generated mostly from interest rate spreads, investing deposits, and borrowings in real estate loans, should be considered "core" earnings, a recurring income source.

Other earnings—gains realized during periods of declining interest rates or from selling mortgages and mortgage-backed securities—should be considered nonrecurring and extraordinary.

The differences between bottom-line reported earnings and core earnings often are significant.

A Case in Point: First Federal of Michigan

First Federal of Michigan, the nation's largest thrift outside of California, reported primary earnings before extraordinary items as $9.61 per share in 1986. Fully diluted earnings after extraordinary items (retirement of high rate Federal Home Loan Bank advances) was reported as $6.26.

But, First Fed's earnings, after extraordinary items, included pretax gains of $9.74 per share on sales of investment securities and loans and mortgage-backed securities.

Such gains would most likely not exist in periods of rising interest rates. Moreover, while First Fed's gains were reported in 1986, it is doubtful all price appreciation occurred during that year.

Golden West Financial Corporation

To their credit, Golden West Financial Corporation, a large California thrift, observed in an annual report that core earnings rather than reported earnings were more important to understand a company's performance. The chart on page 66 is from their 1987 annual report.

Please note that non-core income still remains income and plays a role in establishing the worth of the business. Obviously, however, reported earnings alone cannot possibly help investors

Earnings Per Share

	1987	1986	1985	1984	1983
Reported	4.84	5.89	5.14	2.61	2.50
Core	3.61	3.54	3.23	1.59	1.09

understand the long-term wealth-generating potential of a savings and loan.

PER SHARE EARNINGS

Here are two bits of advice for the value investor. Rule number 1: Don't take a single year's earnings seriously. Rule number 2: If you do, look out for booby traps. Graham said it first, and I agree.

Carefully examine the way per share figures have been obtained; otherwise, the investor will be left in the dark, unable to determine normal earnings and the fair or intrinsic value of the business.

Consider First Fed, cited above. Using too short a time period—where interest rates trend in only one direction, for instance—can mislead investors as to basic earnings and growth potential. It is necessary to consider earnings over a *complete* interest rate cycle.

Use of Average Earnings

Sophisticated investors generally average earnings over fairly long periods—five years or more. This smooths out gyrations of the business cycle and presents a truer picture of earning power. Long-term averaging neatly handles the problem of special charges and credits since they're included in the average.

LOOK FOR HIDDEN ASSETS

Undervalued or hidden assets are an element value investors look for. Keep firmly in mind the fact that corporate assets sometimes go unreflected on balance sheets. Even more important, the market value of these assets may be higher than the stock price itself.

Real estate frequently falls into the undervalued asset category since land is carried at cost and buildings at depreciated cost. Suppose land prices go up? When that happens the *actual* market value can be considerably above *stated* book value.

Stay Home or Go and Look?

Some value investors frequently visit companies to figuratively kick the tires. My own belief is that such visits don't add much and could even subtract from objectivity.

Sufficient data can be mustered from studying the company's financial material as stated earlier. Considerable insight about management's efforts can be obtained simply by reading their ideas and planning. Here are a few guideposts to management that can be discovered in the material:

1. How many new products has the company developed successfully in the past few years?
2. What percentage of last year's sales came from products recently introduced?
3. Is the company diversified?
4. What kind of patent protection or specific know-how protects the company from outside competition?
5. Are they skinflints? How well do they control costs? What "perks" do they take? How much stock do they own?
6. What is the trend of margins?
7. What is the trend of sales and profits?

Staying home is my preference but not everyone is so inclined. Other highly competent value investors insist that site visits are a *must,* although a few, such as Peter Cundill, now do it less and less.

Cundill reasons, "It's more to obtain a physical sense of the business and people, more visceral than anything else." Cundill, it should be noted, frequently takes large positions in companies' shares, often more than 5 percent.

If management interviews make an investor feel more knowledgeable and comfortable, by all means pay a visit. Beware of becoming trapped into giving management double blue chips. This happens when an investor reads and gives good marks to the published material and financial statements and then visits management and gives them good marks for the same things the investor read about. In other words, the investor is counting the good things twice.

WHAT IS MEANT BY FAIR VALUE?

Perhaps now is as good a time as any to define *fair value*.

Fair value is simply the value that rational private business people would pay to buy a whole business, given present interest rates and economic conditions. That is, a price that provides a reasonable rate of return based on the investment in the business.

Perhaps an investor is interested in a business that cost someone $1,000 to set up and now returns $50 annually. That's a lousy rate of return; banks provide better rates.

Suppose, however, the investor pays $500 for the business even though the original guy paid $1,000. The rate of return is better—10 percent.

So, it depends on the rate of return the investor receives on the investment, not whether the business generated a reasonable rate of return.

What causes undervalued stocks to reach fair value? Normal stock market movements in themselves might do it. Or, frequently, some trigger development occurring within the company would cause the stocks to reach fair value. Perhaps a stock repurchase or restructuring or even spinning off an activity; an acquisition, a friendly or unfriendly takeover, or a merger might do it. Keep in mind that undervalued companies are ripe takeover candidates.

Often, too, a business's performance and/or prospects improve and Wall Street takes notice. Graham quotes Horace: "Many shall be restored that now are fallen and many shall fall that now are in honor."

WHAT'S MEANT BY REASONABLE RATE OF RETURN?

That raises another question: What is meant by a *reasonable* rate of return?

The reasonable rate of return has to be a certain premium over current interest rates. That premium depends on several factors, that is, the nature and stability of the business, current economic conditions, and so forth. When purchased at book value, the rates of return on invested capital have averaged 12 percent to 13 percent for the last 50 years.

CASH FLOW CAN BE VITAL

One important part of the financial statements to review is the Statement of Cash Flows. This replaces the old Statement of Changes in Financial Position, effective with fiscal years ended after July 15, 1988. It appears after the income statement and balance sheet in a company's annual and quarterly reports. Using it, the investor can calculate cash flows and observe where funds are coming from and where they are going.

Cash flow can be crucial. A company's cash flow tells whether operations take in more money than the firm spends over a given period. Businesses can lose money and still generate substantial amounts of cash. Net cash generated by the depreciation of plant and inventory on the income statement can go a long way toward keeping a company solvent in rough times.

Temporarily losing money in an accounting sense is acceptable. Even so, beware of chronic negative cash flow. Net free working capital should be sufficient to cover at least three years of negative cash flow.

Study company balance sheets and income statements over a period of several years to provide a more accurate picture of cash flow.

Start with net income before extraordinary items and discontinued businesses and add noncash supplements to working capital, deferred taxes, depletion, amortization, and depreciation. The Financial Accounting Standards Board with the new Statement No. 95 requires that cash flow be divided three ways: operating, investing, and financing cash flow. This will provide a good analytic base for comparing the nature of cash flows and trends and is a welcome improvement.

Price-to-Cash-Flow Ratio

Note that the price-to-cash-flow ratios are calculated similarly to price/earnings ratios by dividing the price per share of the company by the cash flow per share.

For example, Ford Motor had cash flow per share of approximately $16 in 1988. Divided into the price of $51 that results in a price-to-cash flow ratio of slightly more than 3. This compares to the price/cash flow ratio for Honda Motor Co., for example, of 7 1/2.

Looking at price-to-cash-flow ratios can be helpful in comparing some overseas companies to domestic companies.

For example, German accounting allows for large depreciation charges and allocations to reserve accounts, which tend to reduce reported earnings (compared to U.S. GAAP accounting) but not cash flows. Therefore, all other things being equal, it's easier to compare Ford's and Volkswagen's cash flows than reported earnings.

RETURN ON EQUITY

Another useful ratio that can be determined from the financial statements is return on equity—a measure of the rate of return achieved on the assets invested in the business. This ratio is calculated as follows: divide net aftertax income (minus preferred dividends, if any) by the common equity at the beginning of the period (minus goodwill, if any).[1]

If a business has a lot of debt capital, of course, return on equity will be higher than a business without debt, all other things being equal. A business with considerable debt could be riskier than one without debt. So just comparing returns on equity without looking at the nature of the balance sheet could cause grave errors to be made by the investor.

Returns on equity can be useful, however, in determining how profitable and well managed a business is. Kellogg, the world's largest cereal company, in 1986 had a five year average return on equity of 33 percent, a wonderful business.

Over the same period, Royal Nedlloyd Group, the shipping company, had an average return on equity of 5 percent, a not so wonderful business.

Which was the better investment?

Value investors would pick Royal Nedlloyd, as it sold for 25 percent of stockholder's equity (a 20 percent rate of return for new investors in the company at this price) while Kellogg sold at six times shareholder's equity (a 6 percent rate of return to new investors.)

Note that value investors should be looking for high rates of return on equity at reasonable prices. The experienced value investor might pay more than book value (shareholder's equity) for a business generating stable and reasonably sure superior rates of return on equity. The safe course, though, for the less knowledgeable investor, would be to stick to the criteria previously mentioned and buy only when the price is below book value.

CONCLUSION

We've looked at financial statements. It's time to take a hard look at one of the most important questions—when should a stock be sold? For that, we'll turn to Chapter 7.

NOTES

1. Note that if the company has a large deferred tax liability, you might want to add this figure to common equity as it is an interest-free loan from the government that is used as equity.

CHAPTER 7

WHEN TO SELL AND WHEN
NOT TO

There are valid personal reasons why an investor might decide
to sell common stocks: to capitalize a new business; to finance a
new home; or, perhaps, to cope with a sudden catastrophe. This
type of selling, personal rather than financial, falls beyond the
scope of Chapter 7.

Rather, the purpose of Chapter 7 is to cover selling moti-
vated by a single objective—value investing. The chapter
presents three reasons a value investor would find acceptable for
premature selling and also provides assistance in establishing
value selling points. Other portions of Chapter 7 address bear
markets, market appreciation, and price fluctuation. Several
tips and clues have also been provided regarding market un-
certainty and volatility.

THREE REASONS FOR
SELLING PREMATURELY

The value investor generally sells a value stock prematurely
only on three separate occasions:

1. A mistake was made.
2. A better prospect has appeared (rare).
3. The security no longer qualifies as value stock.

Nobody's Perfect

Even the shrewdest of investors occasionally makes a mistake. Analysis is not always perfect, so it may become apparent that the actual condition of a particular company doesn't measure up to the original perception. Handling this type of situation calls for emotional self-control as well as some measure of self-honesty.

Above all, the ego should be kept under control. Sometimes investors fall in love with a stock or feel foolish about being wrong and rationalize that if a "loser" can be sold at a small profit the buy wasn't so dumb. That's normal and natural. But it's also dangerous. Probably more money has been lost by investors who have clung to stocks until they could break even than for any other single reason. So, instead of becoming disgusted or emotionally upset, review each loss with care—a valuable lesson can be learned.

Fortunately, over the long haul, profits obtained from really good value stocks should produce enough gains to more than offset losses from a normal percentage of such mistakes. This is particularly true if the mistake is recognized quickly and then rectified, permitting funds to be freed up for use where substantial gains can be produced.

The Grass Is Greener Theory

The second reason value investors might sell stocks seldom arises. When, and if, it does occur, it should be acted on only when the investor is absolutely certain.

The scenario goes like this. An investor takes a position in a well-run company that is believed to have definite value prospects. Over time, the investor discovers that such value prospects are not as attractive as some other value situation. In this case, the value investor may find it prudent to switch to a better security—but care should be taken. Relative value judgments are difficult. The investor may run the risk of doubling the chances for error—both on the security sold and on the new security purchased.

By this time the reader has probably discovered a basic value principle.

Once a stock has been properly selected and has borne the test of time, it is rare that any reason exists for selling until fair value has been reached.

What about Bear Markets?

The reader may correctly ask: "What about bear markets?" Recommendations and comments pour from the financial community to sell (or, postpone a purchase) because a bad bear market lies just over the horizon. Historically, the market runs in cycles—as will be illustrated in Chapter 13. So, if the company is really all right on all fundamental counts, the next bull market should see it coming back.

Further, if the investor sells the stock with the intention of riding out a bear market and then rebuying the security, the question that rides tandem is: When should the stock be repurchased? Theoretically, repurchase should occur after the decline, which presupposes that the investor knows when the end will come. In fact, experience dictates that investors rarely get back into the same shares until they have greatly increased over the selling price. The October 1987 decline saw many investors dispose of holdings that only six months later showed large positive gains.

Frequently, anticipated bear markets never come. No small amount of truth can be found in a statement of Paul Samuelson, the noted economist, who, when talking about recessions, said: "The market has accurately called nine of the last five recessions." His quip might equally apply to bear market warnings.

Stocks that No Longer Qualify

The third reason for premature selling runs something like the following. Sales should always be made of corporate shares of companies that no longer qualify as value securities under the principles that were outlined earlier.

Look to Minimizing Risk

The above three reasons are the only ones a value investor would accept for selling stocks before they reached a predetermined fair value. Conversely, stocks can be kept indefinitely if (1) the business grows in intrinsic value at a satisfactory rate, and (2) the market doesn't overvalue it.

That means—and this is important—if active markets stopped tomorrow, to be resumed two years hence, a value investor would not be bothered by a lack of quotes. Active trading markets are useful, but by no means essential. They can even be detrimental if their convenience creates improper actions.

Sooner or later the fate of a value stock will be determined by the economic fate of the businesses "owned." The market may ignore business success for a time but eventually will confirm it. And delayed recognition frequently provides the advantage of buying more shares at bargain prices.

CASE OF ROYAL NEDLLOYD

Perhaps another example would better illustrate.

The shares of Royal Nedlloyd Group, a Dutch shipping company, traded at 25 percent of book value, 2 times cash flow, and 6 times earnings. The dividend yield was 8 percent.

Nedlloyd was initially acquired by my firm in 1985 at $35 per share. The company's price later rose to a share price of $90. News came of a Nedlloyd loss for fiscal 1987 as well as a dividend cut. That was followed shortly thereafter by the October 1987 market correction. The company's market price dropped more than 30 percent and my clients grew doubtful. "Why didn't you sell at $90?"

Our research had pegged Nedlloyd's long-term value at $125 to $130 per share: The drop to $60 provided an opportunity to purchase more shares at 50 percent instead of 75 percent of value. Shipping rates then turned around, profitability was restored to Nedlloyd, and we sold our position at $125 per share.

YARDSTICKS FOR SELL POINTS

As the reader can see from the above story, value investors have already established sell points *before* shares are purchased.

Unfortunately, sell points are not fixed and immovable. Frequently they fly off in one of three different directions, so coping with them becomes extremely important.

When Should a Sell Price Be Increased?

A value investor would increase a stock's sell price any time a company reinvests earnings in its business, everything else being the same. (By everything else I mainly mean the rate of return on equity and market value of assets.) Reinvesting in businesses makes sense particularly when the resulting returns are higher than if the earnings were distributed and then reinvested elsewhere. The reason for this is that since a company's fair value has been increased, the sell price also must be readjusted upward—even if the rate of return on the reinvested earnings is low or poor.

Let's turn again to the Royal Nedlloyd Group. For five years the company averaged a 5 percent return on shareholder's equity and reinvested all of its cash flow. That meant the real value of the reinvested money declined, given a 5-percent return. On the other hand, Royal Nedlloyd was priced at 25 percent of book value and therefore generated a 20 percent rate of return for new shareholders.

Perhaps some clarification is in order. By reinvesting the shipping company's earnings, the business only receives a 5 percent return on equity. So every $100 of reinvested earnings in that business is worth considerably less than $100. Management puts in $100, but the value of the company increases much less due to the low rate of return. But it has increased.

Now let's turn to Handy & Harman, the fabricator and refiner addressed in Chapter 6. Although not reported in earnings, sale value of Handy & Harman was raised due to an increase in the underlying market value of its gold and silver inventory which, in turn, increased the intrinsic value of the company. The kind of increase to credit to the company depends on the short-term nature of market swings in the quotational values of gold and silver.

When Does a Sell Price Remain the Same?

In the second scenario, a firm pays out its earnings and everything else remains equal. In this case the sale price remains constant.

When Should a Sell Price Be Lowered?

Sell prices should be lowered if the intrinsic value of a company declines. That could occur for several reasons: a permanent decline in corporate earning power; or, a decline in the rate of return on invested capital from almost any kind of extraneous factor. A semimonopoly position might be lost due to new competition, reducing future basic earnings power. Or, a permanent decline might occur in the assets of a company—such as inventories. Here, both intrinsic value and sell point would decline.

Take, for example, a computer company whose computers and inventories declined in value because some other firm unveiled a faster computer. The first company would have to unload their computers at a lower price. That, in turn, would drop the value of inventory as well as total corporate value.

When Market Price Goes above Fair Value

On the other hand, what happens when something catches the market's fancy and the stock price rises over a company's fair value price? A good question. It happens often, given the nature of the market. The value investor sells when the fair value point is reached and does not try to hold out for the highest price. Conservative value investors recognize that holding a security past the point of fair value strays from investing into speculating. The margin of safety, necessary in case of adverse future developments, has been lost.

For the main, value investors never reproach themselves for selling too soon. Stocks are held so long as the fair value is higher than the stock price.

MARKET FLUCTUATIONS AS A GUIDE

Short-term market fluctuations should become part of a value investor's thinking only on two limited occasions: when the market is so low that a company can be purchased at two thirds of its true worth; and when a stock price approaches true value. Other than that, value investors find market moves of little consequence.

Risk and Uncertainty

Investing by its nature involves an element of risk; something can always go wrong. By working to understand and minimize the risks an investor can achieve acceptable results. By that is meant beating the market from time to time and overall.

The plain truth is no one beats the market *all* the time. One reason for this is that outsiders cannot acquire complete knowledge of a company no matter how many documents are studied or how intimate the relationship has been with management. Another reason would be incorrect analysis, such as failure to account for some crucial factor or a misappraisal of management. The third reason has been emphasized elsewhere in this book: the future cannot be predicted.

Sound and attractive investments fail frequently because management has preempted the intrinsic values for themselves, effecting force-out mergers or similar corporate events when a stock's price is depressed or underpriced.

These previously mentioned uncertainties can never be eliminated. Rather, the goal is to tip the risk-profit equation toward profit as much as possible.

Risk and Volatility

Many Wall Streeters fervently preach that volatility of a stock price equates to risk. Since value investors find that view incorrect, it should therefore be addressed.

From August to October 1987, the stock market fell 983.68 points and sent the Dow Jones Industrial Average from a high of

2,722.42 to a low of 1,738.74. What this means is that the quotational values of American businesses declined. There's a very important distinction between quotational values and actual values. The general perception is that short-term stock quotations reflect the actual value of a business. The majority of the time this is not true.

The wealth of the country didn't change one bit in the October decline. This wealth consists of the businesses themselves plus what they can produce. This has nothing to do with the quotational value from day to day.

An example may place stock price changes into context.

Let's say we have a small company that produces a widget and there are 100 shares outstanding. The $1,000 invested in the company nets on the average $100 after taxes. The stock has an intrinsic value of $10 per share.

Then someone wants a share—perhaps he's had a hot tip—but can't find a seller. He has to offer $50 before someone sells him a share. Along comes another investor, with tax problems, who needs to raise cash fast. He must sell his share but can only get $5 for it on that particular day. The stock price has declined, almost overnight, from an inflated $50 a share to a depressed $5 a share. Does that mean that the company's wealth has almost disappeared or that shareholders' wealth has declined? No. There's no change in either of those. The wealth is the actual value of the company not what *marginal* stock trades are doing.

There's little question that market volatility has increased, mainly from the speed of trading and a largely institutional market. But market fluctuations play a small role in value investing and they do not equate to risk for the long-term value investor.

Risk, for value investors, is an adverse change in the intrinsic value of the business. The idea then is to keep an eye on the company and not the stock price.

What if stock prices decline although nothing substantial has changed? In that case, the investor should consider additional stock purchases. Over the long term, investing in equities at reasonable prices on a diversified basis gives you a higher rate of return than anything else you can possibly invest in—so long as the investor does not panic and sell because of declining stock prices.

CONCLUSION

Chapter 7 presented several guidelines and procedures for eventual sale of value stocks, as well as three reasons a value investor would find acceptable for premature sales. Within the preceding chapters, several ideas were presented concerning specific value stocks. Now let's look at several broad areas into which a value investor might find himself heading. For that, we go to Chapter 8.

CHAPTER 8

INTERESTING HUNTING GROUNDS

The previous chapters have dealt with common stock selection in terms of broad groups of eligible securities. From these groups, a value investor could make up any list that an investor or an adviser might prefer—given adequate diversification.

The emphasis has been chiefly on exclusions, advising on the one hand against most issues of recognizably poor quality, and, on the other hand, against the highest-quality issues if their price is so high as to involve a considerable speculative risk.

Addressed in Chapter 8 are several broad areas into which a value investor might venture as a potential happy hunting ground. Ideally, a value investor would apply various tests of quality and price reasonableness. Also touched on are areas to avoid.

NEW ISSUES

Initial public offerings (IPOs) are not recommended for the average value investor. This isn't so because of the quality of the issue but because of the hoopla and excessive promotion. In the mid-1980s initial public equity offerings were at 15 times earnings—often reaching 25 to 50 times earnings. This is way too high for value investors. With expectations set so high, the odds of disappointment are too great. A value standpoint requires that the investor pay only for what is seen, not what is hoped.

Young public companies shouldn't be dismissed out of hand, however. There is a time to look at them. In most instances, it's after the stock has traded for a period and the initial fanfare has faded. Problems may have arisen in the young company's fortunes: Either management can't handle growth, fails at diversification, expands too rapidly, or competition becomes more intense. Two scenarios might well occur: The stock is richly priced in the offering, rises for a while, then falls back as earnings difficulties arise. Or, the company's stock is overpriced to begin with and immediately falls below the initial offering price.

Bargains can be had for those investors with the patience to look and wait. You should determine, however, whether the problems appear to be temporary and should be rectified eventually.

New Issue Closed-End Funds

The same advice holds true with newly issued closed-end funds. The prudent value investor will avoid them. Purchasing such funds at an initial offering price doesn't make good value sense.

Suppose an investor takes a flyer on a new issue closed-end fund at $12 per share. Chances are a 7.5 percent commission has been tacked on. Right away the net asset value of the fund has dropped to $11.14 per share. If the fund is discounted from net asset value, a common occurrence, the investor is really pushed behind the eight ball.

MERGERS, ACQUISITIONS: TAKEOVER CANDIDATES

Many value-type companies fall into the takeover category. If such a company rests in the investor's portfolio, two questions should be asked: Should you sell out? or, become a minority stockholder?

Selling out avoids any problems. If the value investor elects the other course, examination should be made of the acquiring company to see if it sufficiently warrants being kept in the portfolio as a value stock.

BANKRUPTCY OPPORTUNITIES

Wall Street frequently sneers at bankrupt companies. No matter. Considerable opportunities exist in companies that are sheltered under Chapter 11 of the Federal Bankruptcy Code. (Under Chapter 11 provisions, a company operates with protection from creditors as it attempts to pay its debts.)

Prices of bankrupt companies, generally speaking, are driven down to artificially low levels. Frequently that occurs because financial institutions bail out; it's forbidden for them to hold such securities. Even so, bankrupt companies can prove to be exceptionally good values with large margins of safety. A good example of such a company would be Miller-Wohl. Investors in Miller-Wohl, reorganized in the early 1970s, would have made over 450 times their investment in 10 years. Those purchasing the stocks of Penn Central or Toys "Я" Us have also done well.

The deeply discounted bonds of bankrupt companies are also interesting to value investors. Many of these bonds trade far below the eventual payout upon completion of Chapter 11 proceedings.

Getting the Best Value in Bankrupt Situations

When investigating a bankrupt opportunity, screen for the situation offering a large margin of safety and a reasonably certain outcome. Following are two examples.

Case of Texaco Inc.

Texaco Inc. declared bankruptcy in the spring of 1987 due to the $11 billion judgment awarded Pennzoil by the Texas judicial system.

On the Monday following Texaco's weekend bankruptcy filing, the company's common stock lost 3⅜, 11 percent of market value, as investors fled. The stock price briefly slid from $32 to $27 in one day—down from a yearly high of $47½—and far below an estimated intrinsic value of $60 per share.

The award, $11 billion, was ludicrous and chances were remote Texaco would pay. But, even so, assuming Texaco wound up settling out-of-court for $5 billion ($20 per share), the company's intrinsic value would be $40 per share.

As it happened, within several months, Texaco's stock had recovered into the mid-40s with talk of a compromise settlement with Pennzoil. Even more conservative were Texaco's short-term bonds. The 13 percent notes due August 1, 1991, declined from above par (100) to a low of $79 on the Monday after the Chapter 11 filing. The large cash flow and assets of this company left little doubt that the bonds would be paid off at maturity, even if the entire judgment were upheld.

By the spring of 1988, Texaco had settled out of court with Pennzoil for $3 billion and emerged from Chapter 11. The common stock rose above $50 and the bonds rose as high as 119⅞, reflecting interest to be paid.

Texaco's case illustrates another interesting aspect. With substantial cash flow from operations, the company's value actually grew in bankruptcy due to the cessation of interest and dividend payments.

Case of LTV
When LTV declared bankruptcy in July of 1986, the first mortgage bonds of Jones & Laughlin Steel (which sold as low as $37½) were collateralized by all the land, building, and equipment of the former J & L Steel (now LTV Steel). The depreciated book value of these assets was $296 million, which backed the total claims of the bonds of $315 million—outside appraisers hired by the bond trustees have valued these same assets at $368 million. The bonds now trade at $74 and could be worth $101 or more upon emergence from bankruptcy.

These are only two examples of fine bankruptcy plays. Others will come along occasionally. Do your research and have the patience to wait.

SPECIAL SITUATIONS

Investments that fall under the heading "special situations" can be of merit to value investors if (1) enough information is available for a thorough investigation, and (2) a reasonable rate of return is promised as well as a large margin of safety.

Two current special situation areas would include: (1) liquidations—the selling of all of a business's assets and the distribution of the resulting cash to the shareholders; and (2) arbitrage—cash buyouts in which an offer has been made to purchase all of the common stock of the company for cash.

Examine Liquidations

Liquidations have been a value investor's garden spot for years. That is mainly because the stocks of those businesses that are being liquidated are generally undervalued and inefficiently priced.

One ongoing Florida liquidation illustrates the possibilities available to the value investor. The company is Royal Palm Beach Colony, a Florida real estate developer listed on the American Stock Exchange. Royal Palm's stock trades for $5 per share and, although book value at cost is $2.88 per share, the appraised value of their holdings (mostly land) is nearer $10 per share. Royal Palm's management intends to sell off its properties and then distribute the cash to unit-holders. (This is a partnership.) Complete liquidation could take three years or more. However, as cash becomes available, it is paid out.

Some caveats should be noted. Appraised value does not equal selling price (although sales so far have). Also, Royal Palm's manager has received an incentive for higher sales prices for the land but there is no time limit on this incentive.

At any rate, the margin of safety appears more than adequate. Even more interesting, if liquidation can be completed in three to five years, the rate of return also will be satisfactory.

Look at Arbitrage

Value investors have long been interested in arbitrage situations. Indeed, Benjamin Graham makes a special point of arbitrage in his writings. However, during the past five years the arbitrage community has grown larger. Its growth has been due mainly to the wide assortment of takeover bids that have come down the pike.

Arbitrage issues usually trade about 1 to 5 percent below a

proposed takeover price, reflecting uncertainties over the deal and the wait for the payoff. Arbitrageurs buy with the idea of selling to the takeover company and hope to make 5 percent on capital invested for a few months.

Arbitrage is fairly speculative and certainly not an investment. Occasionally, however, value investors can find opportunities in arbitrage that include an appropriate margin of safety.

How do you take advantage of acceptable arbitrage situations? Scout for large discounts from takeover prices in situations with the following characteristics: (1) friendly offers; (2) financing easy to accomplish; (3) reasonable takeover prices compared to the worth of the business (limiting your downside in the case of noncompletion); (4) expected annualized rate of return at a minimum of 25 to 30 percent; and (5) generally smaller, lesser known buyouts which avoid the competition from risk arbitrage firms and others.

Arbitrage is risky, however. The investor would be acting prudently if no investment was made until after considerable research had been accomplished, following the suggestions previously enumerated.

Two Arbitrage Cases

Several New England savings bank cash buyouts have proved to be interesting arbitrage situations. Two are friendly offers with no financing involved. The cash buyout prices have been no more than 1 to 1.5 times book value, the expected annual rates of return have been over 20 percent, and they have been small issues with no competition from large buyers.

For example, New Bedford Institute for Savings agreed to acquire for cash all the outstanding shares of Taunton Savings Bank of Taunton, Massachusetts, for $17 per share in late 1987. Taunton had a book value of over $14 per share, an equity-to-assets ratio of 23 percent, loan loss provisions practically nil, an average return on equity of 16 percent, and return on assets of 2.37 percent. Other characteristics of this offer met the criteria described above.

The Taunton Savings Bank stock was available at 15¾ per share in April 1988. After regulatory and stockholders' approval, the purchase was completed at $17 in August. The annualized return was approximately 20 percent.

Of nearly one dozen buyouts of New England savings banks within the last year, only one to my knowledge has failed to materialize. That was the purchase of Intrex Financial Services (Lawrence Savings Bank) by Neworld Bancorp at $18.50 per share in cash. Upon Neworld's pullout, the stock of Intrex declined substantially from its quote of $17 per share and now stands at $10 per share. Aspects of this buyout did not meet our previously mentioned criteria but it is a good example of the short-term quotational risk of arbitrage.

JUNK BONDS

Recently we've had the high debt and junk bond phenomenon. So much money has been made in leveraged buyouts and restructuring that the old rules have been forgotten.

The prudent value investor should clearly understand that long-accepted standards for safety in investment grade bonds dictate that for industrial companies earnings before taxes should be five times interest expense. Holding to such a level helps ensure safety in periods of cyclical industry downturns and recessions.

Currently, junk bond issuers have set pre-tax earnings of 1.3 times interest expense as the new standard—and then violated even that.

Case in Point. In attempting to ward off a 1987 takeover, USG Corp. (U.S. Gypsum, the wallboard company) did a leveraged restructuring. The resulting balance sheet now shows negative stockholders' equity of $1.4 billion and long-term debt totaling $2.45 billion. Will this extremely cyclical business earn the more than $290 million per year necessary to pay the interest? Good luck.

Some banks, savings and loans, insurance companies, and mutual funds have jumped aboard the high-yield junk train in a big way. Let's hope the inevitable damage can be held to a minimum. In any case, junk bond issues could be a large future source of opportunities in deeply discounted bankrupt bonds for value investors.

CONCLUSION

The last few chapters have armed you with the fundamentals of value investing. The concepts of screening have been examined, as well as simple rules to follow. Presented also have been value criteria and general guidelines for building a portfolio, how to determine and evaluate value stocks, and some special categories in which bargains may be found.

In the next two chapters, these fundamental concepts are put to work globally. Simple common sense says you'll find more, and sometimes better, investment opportunities by expanding your hunting grounds. The purpose of the next chapter is to help in that search.

In the pages of Chapters 9 and 10, the value investor will gain insight into international investing. Applicable principles, what to examine initially, how to purchase foreign securities effectively, and several significant differences between domestic and foreign markets will be discussed. Mastering international investing requires additional knowledge but is by no means impossible. And the rewards make the effort worthwhile.

CHAPTER 9

HOW TO FIND
OVERSEAS OPPORTUNITIES

An old hand at overseas investing may want to skip the next few pages. But, if cross-border investing is unfamiliar territory, then the average investor might save some pain and money by staying tuned.

Chapter 9 begins by presenting three broad reasons for overseas investing. Later, three different methods are introduced by which value investors might successfully take advantage of foreign opportunities.

WHY INVEST ABROAD?

International portfolio investment has long been a tradition in Europe, but recently there is a growing trend toward it in North America. Value investors have become more willing than ever to send their money across national boundaries mainly for three reasons: the chance for better performance; for greater diversification; and, for more value opportunities.

Market Performance

For the past 10 years, overseas investing has proved exceptionally profitable. A quick glance at performance results of the world's major stock markets starting in 1977 bolsters that belief.

According to Swiss-based Morgan Stanley Capital International, a company which provides statistical and advisory services to major financial institutions around the world, from 1977 to 1987 the number one performing market for each year was: 1977, Britain (up 58%); 1978, France (up 73%); 1979, Norway (up 183%); 1980, Italy (up 81%); 1981, Sweden (up 38%); 1982, Sweden (up 38%); 1983, Italy (up 24%); 1984, Norway (up 82%); 1985, Hong Kong (up 47%); 1986, Austria (up 177%); and 1987, Japan (up 43%).[1]

What about the U.S.? An also-ran: not only did the United States never make it to the top but it managed second place only once during the decade. Never again did it show in the top five.

During 1988 the situation remained almost the same. From January 2 to August 31, total return on U.S. stocks, measured by the S & P 500 Composite Index, turned out to be 8 percent. Again, let's see what happened overseas. Australian equity markets recorded a 32.1 percent gain; the Japanese market rose by 9.1 percent; the Swedish by 17.2 percent; and the Hong Kong market by 9 percent. So performance stories bandied around by overseas investors seem correct—at least, selectively.

Greater Diversification

Diversification, the second reason, simply means the investor does not put all the eggs in one basket. In textbook language, diversification is an attempt to level out market fluctuations and portfolio performance by spreading assets around a number of different industries.

Suppose an investor invested only in companies that supplied health care and prices suddenly dropped throughout that industry. Chances are the investor might be severely affected. But if investments were also made in the auto industry, it's not likely both industries would be hit with simultaneous declines. Investing abroad simply widens the scope of diversification. The investor minimizes market volatility and increases the chances of finding bargains.

This isn't financial pie in the sky, as recent studies by David Brunette and Douglas Stone of the Frank Russell Company, Tacoma, Washington, confirm. The two men matched up the returns of nine major world equity markets and three composite indexes. (The U.S. market was represented by the Russell 3000 Index.) Their findings indicate world markets are only slightly influenced by one another.[2]

For the average value investor, this means that when markets in one region are bubbling it's still possible for good bargains to be found in others.

A World of Value Opportunities

The financial world outside the United States has grown considerably. Not so long ago, American securities markets represented about 67 percent of the value of the entire world's equity markets. Today, that's all changed. Today the United States accounts for 33 percent of the world total. In other words, keeping your investments at home means an investor cuts off 67 percent of the world's investment opportunities.

The enormity of this market has best been put by Lloyds Bank of London which described it thus:

> For a person whose funds are freely transferable, there is a choice of over 50,000 securities available through 20 major stock exchanges throughout the world in 10 important currencies.[3]

The bank's estimate was conservative. If you toss in lesser markets you have 139 stock exchanges in 45 countries.

You may wonder why you had not considered these possibilities before. If the truth be known, until recently most other Americans had not either. That's understandable. Everyone is most familiar with his home turf. Those strangers out there have different customs and languages. And the reverse has held true. "They" haven't come to us either. Foreign investment services have made only half-hearted attempts to capture the U.S. market. Why? A deep aversion to becoming involved with the SEC and other regulatory bodies plus differing securities laws provide the reason.

Despite crossed borders, however, the principles of valuing businesses remain unchanged. So, if a business worth $1 can be purchased for 60 cents, value investors shouldn't care where it's located.

WHERE TO START OVERSEAS

The average value investor can successfully invest overseas using three different methods: (1) prepackaged investments such as discounted closed-end funds, (2) American Depository Receipts (ADRs), or (3) direct purchase of individual shares.

Packaged Overseas Investments

Packaged investments—the funds—could prove a proper ticket even for value investors. By and large, such funds fall into four broad categories: (1) global funds, which invest in all countries, *including* the United States, (2) international funds, which invest in all countries *except* the United States, (3) regional funds, which invest in certain areas, such as Europe or Asia, and (4) single country funds, which invest in one particular country.

Global funds permit investors to totally abdicate decisions as to which countries are most attractive. Their half-brothers, the international funds, remain simply one step up from globals. Both classes were designed for those having neither the time nor inclination to study and research foreign markets and companies. Value investors generally will want more control over where their money is invested. Their focus should be on discounted closed-end regional and single country funds.

Closed-end funds are simply funds where the number of shares outstanding has been fixed. For example, say a new closed-end fund has come to market today, and one million shares are to be sold at $15 per share. That's all the fund plans to issue. A year from now you may want shares in the fund. The price you pay will relate to the fund's net asset value per share *at that time*.

So the fund may sell above this offering price (at a premium) or below it (at a discount). A quick glance at *Barron's,* or a similar publication, tells you no small amount of funds trade at considerable discounts to net asset values. Either way, the fund's position depends strictly on what people think of it. Like other stocks, the fund sells at a price determined by supply and demand.

Now narrow the closed-end concept to closed-end, *single country* funds. They are one smart way to make one-package investments in the securities of such places as Australia, Britain, Brazil, France, Germany, India, Mexico, Malaysia, Switzerland, or Taiwan. Sometimes—such as with Korea—it's the only way. In fact, several closed-end funds invest in smaller countries whose markets are blocked or restricted to non-residents and a fund even exists for emerging markets.

Closed-enders give the investor a number of other significant benefits. The fund's management, for example, takes care of all foreign angles, such as paying taxes, collecting dividends abroad, and converting all foreign income into dollars. The funds are priced in dollars and dividends are paid in dollars.

Imagine a new fund comes on the market at $12 a share and in a matter of months reaches $80 per share, a 200 percent premium over net asset value. If you sell at that price you have made almost seven times your money. This may be impossible for a mutual fund, of course, but not for a closed-end fund like the Korea Fund, which achieved those figures from mid-1984 to mid-1985. Incidentally, I sold my position in the Korea Fund when it reached its intrinsic net worth level of 16⅝.

How to Pick a Fund

Selecting the appropriate fund is not that difficult. First, write a fund and request its shareholder information. Then weave what you receive together with information culled from either *Barron's* or *The Wall Street Journal* reports. Here's what you would learn if you did this with the funds listed below.

1. *The Germany Fund,* with assets of about $60 million, was started in 1986 and has a wide spread of German stocks, mainly in insurance, retail, electrical, chemical, and automotive companies. The 10 largest equity holdings of the Germany Fund as of June 30, 1988, included the following: BASF; Bayer; Allianz Holding; Feldmuhle Noble; Thyssen; Commerzbank; Dresdner Bank; Daimler-Benz; Siemens AG; and Bayerische Hypotheken und Wechsel-Bank AG.

2. *The Mexico Fund,* with assets of about $140 million, has a portfolio of about two dozen Mexican companies, with some 40 percent of its portfolio in chemical, construction, and mining shares, all of which are heavy exporters to the United States and thus receive a large part of their revenues in dollars. Mexico has had some well-publicized economic problems including $100 billion in foreign debt and a large, volatile inflation rate. At this writing, the Mexico Fund is a good value fund, offering value investors a 35 percent discount while the average Mexican stock trades at six times earnings.

3. *The Templeton Emerging Markets Fund,* with assets of about $100 million, traded initially on the American Stock Exchange in March 1987 and rose to an 18.4 percent premium in barely a month. It now sells at a 17 percent discount. The Emerging Markets Fund is managed by John Templeton's organization—a very experienced and successful global value investor. Its goal is to achieve long-term appreciation of capital by investing in the stocks of 42 emerging countries, even some Communist countries, such as Communist China and Yugoslavia. Included in the Emerging Markets' portfolio are the following issues: Hongkong and Shanghai Banking Corp.; Swire Pacific Ltd.; Philippine Long Distance Telephone Company; Paterson Zochonis P.L.C.; Cable and Wireless P.L.C.; Industrial Finance Corporation of Thailand; Cheung Kong (Holdings) Ltd; Polly Peck International P.L.C.; Oceans Wilsons (Holdings) P.L.C.; and Compagnie Francaise de l'Afrique Occidentale.

Use a Two-Step Decision-Making Process

Now we are ready for some practical details. Which fund to buy? How do you find information on fund discounts? On fund premiums?

The smart way is to divide the decision making process into two stages.

Step 1. Check the latest weekly table of premiums and discounts in the financial press. Select the funds with the widest discounts. Look in a weekly table published under the heading "Publicly Traded Funds" in Monday's *The Wall Street Journal* or "Closed-End Stock Funds" in *Barron's* or the *Los Angeles Times* and other newspapers.

Here is a sampling of some current closed-end fund discounts as of December 1988—all of which value investors might examine: ASA Ltd, NYSE, 29 percent discount to net asset value; Asia Pacific, NYSE, a 28 percent discount; Mexico Fund, NYSE, a 34 percent discount; Scudder New Asia, NYSE, a 25 percent discount; and Brazil Fund, NYSE, a 34 percent discount.

Remember, fund prices swell and shrink just like those of individual businesses, so pay careful attention to the discounted variety. Exhibit 9-1 duplicates the listing found in *Barron's* each week. Check back copies of those periodicals to see if the discount has been larger in the past than now. It may sink to lower levels again. (In July 1988, the Mexico Fund registered a 28 percent discount.)

A few paragraphs back, discounts registered by several closed-end funds were flagged. Interestingly enough, each was discounted greater than 20 percent. There's a reason. An important cutoff rule for selecting the right closed-end funds is to look for at least a 20 percent discount to net asset value. Granted, that rule isn't hard and fast, but keep it in mind when scouring financial pages and the closed-end fund table.

How else does the table help? Say an investor is interested in Mexican opportunities and believes that the nation's economic woes will disappear and that Mexican stocks are now bargains. Still, a direct purchase seems too risky. A quick check through the line on the table shows that the Mexico Fund trades on the NYSE. That by itself indicates that the Fund has passed two rigorous but comforting examinations: the SEC's eagle eye plus the entrance requirements for NYSE listing. Also, you'll discover the Fund's net asset value is 8.29 and that it sells at 5½—a 34 percent discount. In other words, the Mexico Fund's a potential bargain.

Consider the opportunities available. If the fund's discount shrinks and eventually reaches net asset value, or if the dollar drops against the foreign currency involved, or if the foreign stock market climbs, you are going to come out ahead.

By following the procedure outlined above, you'll probably locate several funds with attractive-looking discounts.

Step 2. Next, direct your attention and thinking to the value guidelines which were outlined earlier. Read the fund's prospectus and how it operates, but make certain your informa-

EXHIBIT 9-1
Barron's Closed-End Funds (October 24, 1988)

Fund Name	Stock Exch.	N.A. Value	Stock Price	% Diff.
Specialized Funds				
1st Australian	AMEX	10.95	8½	− 22.37
1st Iberian	AMEX	9.48	7¾	− 18.25
ASA Ltd-b c	NYSE	52.98	39	− 26.39
American Capital Conv-a	NYSE	23.18	23⅜	+ 0.84
Asia Pacific	NYSE	8.48	6⅛	− 27.77
BGR Prec Metals-b e	TOR	12.58	10⅜	− 17.53
Bancroft Convertible-g	AMEX	23.19	18⅜	− 20.76
Brazil	NYSE	12.56	9⅝	− 23.37
CNV Holdings Capital	NYSE	9.03	4⅝	− 48.78
CNV Holdings Income	NYSE	9.40	11¼	+ 19.68
Castle Convertible-a	NYSE	21.83	20	− 8.38
Central Fund Canada-b	AMEX	5.94	5¼	− 11.62
Central Securities	NYSE	11.79	10	− 15.18
Claremont Capital	NYSE	54.10	52¾	− 2.50
Counsellrs Tandem Secs	NYSE	8.49	6⅜	− 24.91
Cypress Fund	NYSE	9.36	7¼	− 22.54
Duff & Phelps Sel Utils	NYSE	7.98	8⅜	+ 4.95
Ellsworth Conv Gr&Inc	NYSE	8.75	7½	− 14.29
Engex Inc.	AMEX	13.25	10	− 24.53
Financ'l News Compos	NYSE	17.00	14	− 17.65
First Financial Fund	NYSE	9.18	7½	− 18.30
France Fund-b	NYSE	11.15	9⅛	− 18.16
Gabelli Equity Trust	NYSE	11.27	9⅞	− 12.38
Germany Fund	NYSE	8.27	7⅝	− 7.80
H&Q Healthcare Inv	NYSE	8.02	6¼	− 22.07
Hampton Utils Tr Cap-b	AMEX	10.07	8⅜	− 16.83
Hampton Utils Tr Pref-b	AMEX	48.42	46½	− 3.97
Helvetia Fund	NYSE	11.40	9⅝	− 15.57
India-f	NYSE	11.96	9⅛	− 23.70
Italy Fund-b	NYSE	z	z	z
Korea Fund	NYSE	13.83	23⅜	+ 69.02
MG Small Cap	NYSE	8.82	7½	− 14.97
Malaysia Fund	NYSE	9.03	7⅜	− 18.33
Mexico Fund-b	NYSE	7.40	4⅞	− 34.12
Petrol & Resources	NYSE	26.70	23⅜	− 12.45
Pilgrim Reg Bk Shrs	NYSE	10.03	8¼	− 17.75
Real Estate Sec & Inc	AMEX	9.18	9⅛	− 0.60
Regional Fin Shrs Inv	AMEX	8.10	6½	− 19.75
Scandinavia Fund	NYSE	8.56	6⅝	− 22.61
Scudder New Asia	NYSE	11.55	8⅝	− 25.32
Spain Fund	NYSE	11.35	9⅝	− 15.20
TCW Convertible Secs-b	NYSE	8.20	7⅞	− 3.96
Taiwan Fund-b	NYSE	31.28	27⅞	− 10.89
Templeton Emerg Mkts-b	NYSE	9.45	8⅛	− 14.02
Thai Fund	NYSE	11.54	12⅝	+ 9.40
United Kingdom Fund	NYSE	11.60	9⅜	− 19.18
Z-Seven-d	NYSE	14.19	15	+ 5.71

a-Ex-dividend. b-As of Thursday's close. c-Translated at Commercial Rand exchange rate. d-NAV reflects $2.66 per share for taxes. e-In Canadian Dollars. f-As of Wednesday's close. g-Subject to adjustment for rights offering. n-Nasdaq National Market System. p-Pacific Exchange. z-Not available.

tion is up-to-date; funds can and do change investing strategies. Examine the fund's portfolio for value stocks; see if a highly recognized stock selector is making the choices. What has the fund's record been over the past five years? A superior past doesn't guarantee future results. Investing overseas can be tricky. Many fund managers are unfamiliar with foreign waters and their newly acquired understanding could be at your expense.

Watch for Traps

A few paragraphs ago I advocated a 20 percent, or greater, discount guide for initial value screening. Even with that guideline your purchase still could wind up being a Faustian bargain.

Here's why. Scudder's New Asia Fund, to take an example, currently offers a 25 percent discount. That much discount seemingly meets value criteria. Even so, some of the fund's securities may come from superheated areas, such as Japan, so you might consider investigating better values elsewhere.

How Do You Buy Closed-End Funds?

Check with your broker. Be prepared for the likelihood that he doesn't know about closed-enders, he doesn't care about them, nor does he have them high in his priorities; not if he can sell you a load mutual fund that brings in a substantial commission.

Here we have one last word on funds. Suppose you've no intention of investing in a closed-end fund. Write for their latest reports anyway. You'll find them useful for information when you buy individual foreign stocks either through ADRs or directly.

TWO OTHER METHODS

As a value investor, perhaps you're highly experienced with funds and have enough energy, ambition, and background to gather information yourself. The next two sections will get you off on the right foot. The first presents an argument for American Depository Receipts (ADRs). The second portion addresses the direct purchase of overseas value stocks.

Use of American Depository Receipts (ADRs)

Stocks of hundreds of foreign companies are available on major U.S. exchanges and can be purchased for dollars like any other stock—through ADRs.

During the 1980s, the popularity of ADRs snowballed. Although 25 years ago only 150 ADRs were available for investors, today the number approximates 750. Some 2 billion ADR shares traded through the New York, American, and NASDAQ mechanisms during 1986, a number that doubled by the end of 1987.

Let us state some basic facts. ADRs aren't actually shares but share stand-ins that entitle holders to all dividends and capital gains that accrue to the share. Also, ADRs can be traded just like underlying shares. They're negotiable receipts issued by American banks such as Citicorp or Morgan Guaranty, an ADR pioneer. Even though receipts, however, ADRs can be converted into a specified number of underlying common shares by notifying the depository bank, who'll charge a small fee for the conversion.

Usually ADRs represent single shares, but not always. If a foreign company's stock price is either relatively low or relatively high in U.S. dollars, then ADRs are handled differently. Issuance comes in units that represent either fractions or multiple shares of the stock.

The ADR mechanism means that investors can operate at home, using familiar rules, and protected by the sheriff—that is, the SEC and other regulatory authorities.

ADRs can be either sponsored or unsponsored. Sponsored ADRs, complying with all SEC reporting requirements, are by far the easiest for the average investor to investigate. Unsponsored ADRs are created by banks that see a profitable market for a particular company's shares.

Why the popularity upsurge? Simplicity is one reason. ADRs cut through most problems found with overseas investing.

Language barriers are avoided since annual reports and other shareholder correspondence are printed in English. Issuers of *listed* ADRs must also provide financial reporting comparable to that of American companies. This means that the investor can quickly compare ADR holdings with domestic alternatives.

There are other bonuses. ADRs frequently prove cheaper due to transaction and other costs. For example, the transaction costs associated with the direct purchase of German stocks can at times be more expensive than those associated with a German company's ADR purchased on the American Stock Exchange. Moreover, dividends are paid to the depository bank which deducts foreign withholding taxes, converts them to dollars, and forwards the balance to the security owner.

How do you purchase ADRs? Simply call a broker. Most any U.S. broker will do. You don't have to deal through foreign brokers or banks.

Direct Dealing Overseas

Given telephone lines, satellites, and electronic linkages, today's cross-border financial factories are open 24 hours a day. So, if an investor has reached an investing level that includes ample time and energy, a case may be built for plunging into direct investments. Here choices expand—a full 50,000 or more securities trade on more than 100 stock exchanges in more than 36 countries around the globe.

Fortunately, an easy way exists to break this group into easy-to-digest, manageable, chunks. The first step is to examine major world markets normally—then as value investors. There's a vast difference.

Again our tour guide is Morgan Stanley who annually reveals how the foreign pie has been divided. Exhibit 9–2, summarizing market shares, shows how the list looked at the end of 1987.

Japan's portion, somewhat skewed, reflects "inflated" values that currently permeate Japanese trading. Now that Japan is the world's biggest, and number-one, stock market, the Japanese currently see stocks bought and sold at a hyperbullish 60 times earnings. More than 100 stocks trade at P/E ratios of

EXHIBIT 9-2
Foreign Markets Share

Europe, Australia, Far East: 64%
United States: 33%

Breaking Europe, Australia, and the Far East down further:
Japan: 40%
United Kingdom: 9%
Germany: 3%
Canada: 2.5%
France: 2.3%
Switzerland: 1.8%
Italy: 1.7%
Netherlands: 1.4%
Australia: 1.3%
Spain: 1%

---

more than 1000, and the Dow Nikkei Exchange hovers around 28,000. By comparison, the average stock in the United States trades at a P/E ratio of 13.

The world securities markets have their "top ten" as far as performance goes, and Exhibit 9-3 shows the list at the end of August 1988. Notice the ranking has been done in "normal" fashion. That is, best performance is ranked number one. Value investors almost reverse the ranking, similar to the right-hand column. Incidentally, the value investor is cautioned to take into account price to book value, price to cash flow, and price to earnings and yield.

The reason for the differences in ranking addresses a significant value guideline: Value bargains generally aren't found in strong markets. A good rule is to examine stock markets that have reacted adversely for a year or so.

For example, during 1987, many growth stock investors and short-term traders zeroed in on the superheated Tokyo Exchange. For many value investors, however, German issues were the rage. Why? During 1987 German stocks dropped 40 percent overall and came up with the worst performance of all world markets—but also presented the best opportunities.

So the game for value investors was to discover which horse to bet on—which German companies met Graham's earlier discussed procedures and criteria. As it happened, two were discovered which will be discussed later.

EXHIBIT 9-3
Foreign Market Performance*

Normal Ranking†	Value Investor Ranking*
1. Australia	1. The Netherlands
2. Japan	2. Germany
3. Canada	3. Switzerland
4. U.S.A.	4. France
5. France	5. United Kingdom
6. Spain	6. Spain
7. The Netherlands	7. U.S.A.
8. Germany	8. Canada
9. United Kingdom	9. Australia
10. Switzerland	10. Japan

* January 31, 1988 to August 31, 1988
† Morgan Stanley Capital International Perspective

SELECTING YOUR STOCKS

How does the value investor find overseas value stocks? How do you determine true value in foreign issues? Which do you choose?

The obvious advice is you should do a thorough job of boning up. Study foreign gross national products, read tax legislation, go over everything you can concerning economic futures, business conditions abroad, and the outlook for overseas stock markets. Attend lectures, read foreign newspapers, and so forth. Don't plan on allotting a few minutes a week for this purpose; this is time consuming.

Actually all this is unnecessary because you just want to select individual businesses to study, not the global economy. Now I'll show you some resources to make that task easier.

Use of Morgan Stanley's *Capital International Perspective*

One such resource is Morgan Stanley's *Capital International Perspective* which can be a fertile hotbed of foreign investment ideas.

Morgan Stanley's periodical is an astonishingly compact

source of financial data, complete with text and logarithmic charts that are broken down by country and industry group.

Let's say that Holland has caught your eye in general and KLM in particular. Here's some of the information you can pick up in just a few minutes by reading Morgan Stanley's periodical from which an excerpt has been duplicated in Exhibit 9–4.

Case of KLM

The line on KLM identifies the company as a Dutch stock that is 39 percent government owned. The periodical also notes KLM's market value is $838 million (in dollars), price to book value is .57:1, price divided by cash earnings (reported earnings plus depreciation of fixed assets) is 2.1:1, and price to earnings is 4.8:1. Book value is FL 2.6 billion and the dividend yield is 5.5 percent as of December 31, 1987. Charts in the periodical tell you that KLM traded in 1987 for around FL25 to FL58 and closed at the end of 1987 at FL29. For the past five years, KLM has traded between FL16 and FL68. It traded as low as FL7 in the mid-1970s and as high as FL90 in 1967. KLM's ADR ticker symbol is KLM. It is categorized under a subgroup of transportation issues—airlines.

The company has paid a dividend since 1985, with dividends of FL1.60 per share paid during both 1987 and 1986. The company has fixed assets of FL5.6 billion, current assets of FL3.7 billion, current liabilities of FL2 billion, long-term liabilities of FL3.7 billion, and other liabilities (such as pension plans, deferred taxation, minority interests) of FL1.4 billion. Capital is 51 million shares outstanding. Earnings for the past five years were: 1987, FL5.92; 1986, FL6.14; 1985, FL7.35; 1984, FL2.69; and 1983, FL2.02. Recent information includes load factors for fiscal 1986, 66.9 percent and for fiscal 1987, 70.7 percent.

Another Way to Birddog

Pick up the latest quarterly reports from a closed-end mutual fund similar to one of those mentioned earlier. Fund reports provide a wealth of material for investment ideas. What's more, the investor will also find foreign stock market data as well as knowledge on particular foreign companies.

EXHIBIT 9–4
KLM

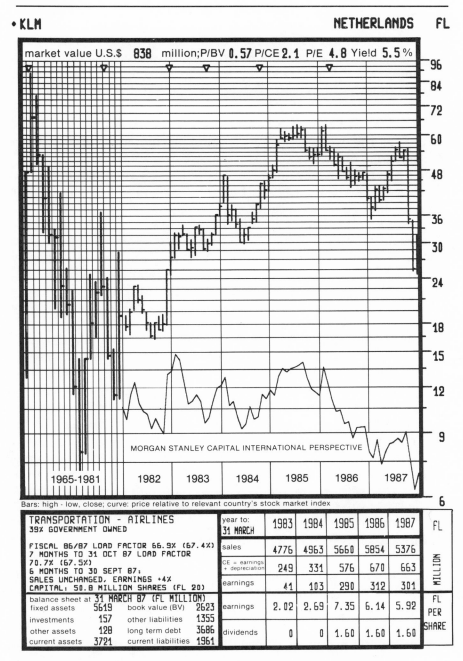

• KLM   **NETHERLANDS   FL**

market value U.S.$ **838** million;P/BV **0.57** P/CE **2.1** P/E **4.8** Yield **5.5**%

Bars: high - low, close; curve: price relative to relevant country's stock market index

MORGAN STANLEY CAPITAL INTERNATIONAL PERSPECTIVE

1965-1981   1982   1983   1984   1985   1986   1987

TRANSPORTATION - AIRLINES
39% GOVERNMENT OWNED

FISCAL 86/87 LOAD FACTOR 66.9% (67.4%)
7 MONTHS TO 31 OCT 87 LOAD FACTOR
70.7% (67.5%)
6 MONTHS TO 30 SEPT 87:
SALES UNCHANGED, EARNINGS +4%
CAPITAL: 50.8 MILLION SHARES (FL 20)

balance sheet at **31 MARCH 87 (FL MILLION)**

fixed assets	5619	book value (BV)	2623
investments	157	other liabilities	1355
other assets	128	long term debt	3686
current assets	3721	current liabilities	1961

year to: 31 MARCH	1983	1984	1985	1986	1987	FL
sales	4776	4963	5660	5854	5376	MILLION
CE = earnings + depreciation	249	331	576	670	663	
earnings	41	103	290	312	301	
earnings	2.02	2.69	7.35	6.14	5.92	FL PER SHARE
dividends	0	0	1.60	1.60	1.60	

Source: *Morgan Stanley Capital International Perspective*, January 1988, p. 432.

Consider the Germany Fund's quarterly report. Issued August 10, 1988, the report provides investors with German economic data. Thumbnail sketches are provided of many companies held including BASF and Siemens AG.

Consider BASF and Siemens AG

BASF is the world's largest chemical company, producing a broad range of chemicals, dyes, plastics, and fertilizers. In 1987, some 64 percent of the company's sales came from outside Germany. The company's U.S. subsidiaries include the former Inmont and American Enka.

Siemens AG is one of the world's leading electrical/electronics producers, and Germany's fourth largest company in terms of sales. It manufactures a broad and technologically sophisticated range of products oriented toward growth areas in electrical engineering. In the United States, the company's second most important sales market, Siemens AG is particularly strong in medical engineering systems.

Meanwhile, the financial information in *Capital Perspective* says essentially that both BASF and Siemens AG seemingly meet value stock criteria.

So here are two interesting investment ideas on which to follow up. (This is only an initial screening, of course. Additional work needs to be done, examining the companies' financials and the nature of the business.)

Keep in mind, however, that your main interest is to scout out value gems. Ask yourself *what is the stock, anywhere in the world, that sells at the lowest price in relation to what its value is estimated to be?*

Follow Value Principles

The value investor should absolutely eliminate consideration of any company not meeting the same criteria as domestic firms discussed earlier: below book value; low price-earnings ratio; high dividend yield; price/cash-flow ratio, and so forth. Review the company's assets, especially such liquid assets as cash, inventories, and receivables, either on or off the books. Then compare this amount to corporate liabilities. Also, review the price-earnings streams or other financial characteristics and compare liquidation value to current stock price and the rate of return on stockholder's equity.

Reading between the Lines Pays Off

Earlier we discussed reading how value investors change market rankings. Value investors also read between the lines, especially when examining Fund reports.

In 1987, Scandinavia Fund president Bjorn Carlson noted his fund had dumped its Norwegian investments. The reason? The Norwegian economy had been hurt both by the fall in the price of oil, its major export, and a rising inflation rate. That news in itself was only a blip squeezed among pages of economic and fund data, but it graphically demonstrates how perceptions differ between short-term traders and value investors.

Most short-term traders would take Mr. Carlson's data as a key clue to head elsewhere; value investors would react differently.

My reaction was to open *Capital Perspective* to see if a Norwegian horse was available for the next race—one wearing value colors. As it happened, the Bergen Bank proved a likely candidate. The Bergen Bank at year-end 1987 traded for 67 percent of book value and 4 times earnings. The bank's dividend yield was 10.3 percent. Bergen Bank seemed interesting enough for a look-see.

Obtaining the bank's annual report was the next step, mainly to examine the financials and accounting. They proved even more interesting. Even after accounting adjustments and taxes the stock was greatly underpriced. Unfortunately, the daydreams shattered upon discovery of a 50 percent premium required for share purchase. Too rich!

Incidentally, Bergen Bank's premium existed because of a restriction as to the percentage of foreign ownership allowed by Norway. The premium has varied over the past few years and has disappeared at times. Perhaps it will again.

How to Manage Overseas Trading

The investor can minimize overseas investing difficulties by having an American broker act as go-between in setting up trading arrangements. These brokers are seasoned veterans at foreign trade. Costs are not small, but they ensure that the broker will get you around custodial hassles. You can leave the shares with the broker in "street name", which simply means that your shares would be held in the broker's name instead of yours.

The investor can also contact a foreign investment banking firm like Australia's J.B. Were and London's Barclays de Zoete Wedd.

Finally, if the investor is a healthy customer of a foreign bank ("healthy" means six figures or more), cross-border security deals will be handled as a matter of course.

CONCLUSION

Chapter 9 has presented several arguments in favor of overseas investing, including performance, diversification, and opportunities. Also discussed were discounted closed-end funds, American Depository Receipts, and direct purchase—three methods that the average investor can use to participate in foreign markets. Methods by which the direct investor can minimize custodial problems were noted. Guidelines were presented on how to view world markets as a value investor and how to select value shares.

Overseas investing, however, is not yet a well-oiled machine. Considerable differences exist of which the average investor should be aware. Those differences will be addressed in Chapter 10.

NOTES

1. Percentage change in stock market indices with net dividend yields added back. Adjusted for foreign exchange fluctuations of the relevant currency relative to the U.S. dollar.
2. Frank Russell Co., Tacoma, WA, March 1988. Correlations of returns of major world equity markets have stayed relatively low during the past few years and well within historical levels. The

correlation coefficient measures the degree to which two variables, in this case, market returns, move together. Correlation coefficients vary between 1, meaning the two markets are perfectly positively correlated and -1, indicating a perfectly negative correlation. If the correlation coefficient is zero, markets show no tendency to follow each other. Generally, correlations under 0.75 indicate a weak positive relationship between markets. Correlations for rolling periods that include October, 1987, generally were only slightly higher than correlations calculated for periods that exclude October, 1987. The correlation between the returns of U.S. and foreign stocks is $+0.67$. Since the correlation is less than $+1$, international investors lower volatility by adding foreign equities to their portfolios.

3. David Smyth, *Worldly Wise Investor* (New York: Franklin Watts, 1988).

APPENDIX: HOW TO OBTAIN INFORMATION ON OVERSEAS COMPANIES

However you decide to handle trading, you'll want to tap in on information that affects your company. Certain news outlets exist, although you may have to consult more than one.

The Wall Street Journal carries daily quotes on about 400 foreign stocks. The *Journal* also circulates two regional editions abroad: *The Asian Wall Street Journal* and *The Wall Street Journal Europe.* As might be expected, the *Journal*'s regionals carry more regional and international news than the main editions.

The *New York Times* and *Barron's* are other possible sources.

The *Financial Times of London* carries the daily quotations of the entire London Stock Market list, about 600 U.S. stocks and 600 or so other foreign securities. These publications provide daily or weekly quotations on close to a thousand foreign stocks plus the entire London Stock Exchange list.

For the Tokyo Stock Exchange, subscribe to the English-language *Japan Times* or the *Japan Stock Journal.*

If you're high-tech minded, Wright Investor's Services, Bridgeport, CT, offers a computer database service called Worldscope. Worldscope features the world's major corporations, 2,000 American and 2,000 foreign companies based in 24 countries.

Nikkei, Japan's leading economic daily, publishes an English-language version and provides Nikkei Telecom, a database on Japan and Japanese financial markets, as well as Quick, an online system for Japanese market quotes.

A word of caution . . .

Even while several good sources have been listed above, obtaining information on foreign companies can be challenging.

Publicly owned U.S. companies publish their quarterly earnings within a few weeks after the quarter ends. In contrast, certain European or Far Eastern firms only publish earnings once a year. Earnings of French companies, also, become somewhat outdated since earnings are not usually published until six months after the end of the fiscal year. On the other hand, British and Japanese firms publish frequently.

Contacting the companies at their foreign headquarters is essential. Ask for annual and interim reports to shareholders and any other information distributed by the company. Practically all major overseas companies and many smaller ones provide reports in English. The SEC reports (10-K, and so forth), of course, will not be available.

Fortunately, many foreign brokers, and some domestic brokers with overseas operations, have started to provide information on individual companies from a large number of countries. Similarly, data services such as Extel, DAFSA, and Moody's are extending their international coverage of companies and currently feature summary financial information on an increasing number of foreign corporations. Remember that a good deal of opinion is expressed as fact so be sure you form your own opinion along value principles.

Listed below are names and addresses of a few closed-end funds that specialize in overseas issues:

ASA Ltd., NYSE
P.O. Box 39
Chatham, NJ 07928

Asia-Pacific Fund, NYSE
1 Seaport Plaza
New York, NY 10292

Central Fund of Canada,
AMEX
P.O. Box 7319
Ancaster, Ontario 19
L9G 3N6

First Australia Fund, AMEX
1 Seaport Plaza
New York, NY 10292

France Fund, NYSE
535 Madison Avenue
New York, NY 10022

Germany Fund, NYSE
40 Wall Street
New York, NY 10005

Global Growth Fund, NYSE
1 Seaport Plaza
New York, NY 10292

Helvetia Fund, NYSE
10 Hanover Square
New York, NY 10005

Israel Investors Corp., OTC
10 Rockefeller Plaza
New York, NY 10020

Italy Fund, NYSE
2 World Trade Center
New York, NY 10048

Korea Fund, NYSE
345 Park Avenue
New York, NY 10154

Malaysia Fund, NYSE
P.O. Box 9011
Princeton, NJ 08540

Mexico Fund, NYSE
477 Madison Avenue
New York, NY 10022

Taiwan Fund, AMEX
111 Devonshire Street
Boston, MA 02109

Templeton Emerging
Markets Fund, AMEX
700 Central Avenue
St. Petersburg, FL 33701

United Kingdom Fund,
NYSE
55 Water Street
New York, NY 10041

Worldwide Value Fund,
NYSE
7 East Redwood Street
Baltimore, MD 21202

CHAPTER 10

FOREIGN DIFFERENCES

The methods and data required to analyze foreign companies are quite similar to those used for domestic companies. Even so, the international investor faces a complex task. The financial markets throughout the world are quite different from each other. Different accounting principles are used and, even where the same accounting methods are practiced the numbers can be deceptive. Hazardous, also, are many cultural, institutional, political, and tax differences.

Not all overseas investors face such constraints. Investing by the closed-end fund methods previously outlined is perhaps the easiest way of avoiding such complications. Those choosing to go the ADR route will face fewer obstacles, except for accounting practices, than those who plan to invest directly.

The purpose of Chapter 10 is to address several of the complexities and factors that the average overseas value investor must take into account. Because the rules vary so much from country to country, broad guidelines cannot be formulated. Even so, addressing differences that exist in specific countries such as West Germany, Sweden, The Netherlands, Japan, and Australia, will perhaps furnish the average investor with an idea of what to keep in mind. Presented also will be guidelines on how to approach such differences. The objective, of course, is still to detect relative misvaluation, that is, stocks that are bargain issues based upon value criteria. Without some background, the average investor may significantly misjudge the value qualities of an overseas issue.

FINANCIAL DIFFERENCES

Value investors should stay alert to key differences in foreign accounting. Exhibit 10–1 illustrates some of those differences. Steps have been taken to bring more uniformity, but, at the present time, nothing has been finalized.

Foreign accounting mainly tends to be conservative, especially when income or earnings are involved. A case in point is Volkswagen, who, in 1982–83, reported corporate losses of DM 5.23 per share. As a result, Volkswagen's share price dropped. Two years later investors learned that German accounting had misled them. What would have been the amount under U.S. Generally Accepted Accounting Principles (GAAP) methodology? A DM 14.37 per share *profit*—a difference of DM 19.60—solely the result of different accounting practices.

Such disparities result partly from different national tax incentives and the creation of "secret" reserves—often up to 100 percent of fixed assets—to economize on taxes.

West Germany

In examining German firms (and some Swiss firms) an investor should clearly understand that, by U.S. practices, German firms overestimate contingent liabilities and future uncertainties. Inventories are generally understated for tax reasons and are not revalued when prices increase. Mergers and takeovers are reported in the balance sheet based on the book value, not the actual transaction price. That lowers the reported value of equity. The reason for these differences is that German shareholder reports also serve for tax purposes. Since corporations wish to reduce taxable earnings, they understate true economic earnings compared to similar American or English reports.

Suppose a value investor believes a West German issue to be a bargain. Since German earnings are generally understated the next question to pose becomes: by how much?

A good example comes from Siemens AG. Siemens listed a $3.5 billion item under unspecified "other costs" in its 1986 financial statement. This unexplained amount was four times

EXHIBIT 10–1

International Accounting Differences—Selected Accounting Principles

Accounting Principle	Country									
	Australia	Canada	France	West Germany	Japan	Netherlands	Sweden	Switzerland	United Kingdom	United States
Goodwill amortized?	YES	YES	YES	NO	YES	MIXED	YES	NO*	NO*	YES
Provision for bad debts?	YES	YES	NO	YES	YES	YES	YES	YES	YES	YES
Discount/premium on long-term debt amortized?	YES	YES	NO	NO	YES	YES	NO	NO	NO	YES
Long-term financial leases capitalized?	NO	YES	NO	NO	NO	NO	NO	NO	NO	YES
Straight line depreciation adhered to?	YES	YES	MIXED	MIXED	MIXED	YES	YES	YES	YES	YES
Currency translation gains or losses reflected in current income?	MIXED	YES	MIXED	MIXED	MIXED	NO	MIXED	NO(1)	NO	YES
Financial statements reflect historical cost valuation (no price level adjustment)	NO	YES	NO	YES	YES	NO*	NO	NO	NO	YES
Supplementary inflation-adjusted financial statements provided?	NO*	NO*	NO	NO	NO	NO*	NO	NO*	YES	YES

KEY:
YES = The predominant accounting principle
NO = The accounting principle is not adhered to
* = Some exceptions
MIXED = Alternative practices followed with no majority
(1) = Translation gains or losses are deferred

Source: Frederick D.S. Choi and Vinod B. Bavishi, "Diversity in Multinational Accounting." Used by permission from *Financial Executive,* August 1982, copyright 1982 by , Financial Executives Institute.

its profits and three times its tax bill. Conclusion? The investor should investigate these costs as they may be exaggerated; true earnings may be considerably higher.

Several West German companies write off up to 75 percent of the cost of buildings during the first year (in contrast to the typical 5 percent diminishing balance basis for tax reporting and the 20- and 30-year life assumption for Canadian financial reporting.

Sweden

Similarly, Sweden offers corporations favorable tax write-offs within a system of high marginal tax rates. The investor may find seeming distortion, compared to GAAP, simply due to Swedish tax incentives such as accelerated depreciation, inventory write-off, and other provisions.

The Netherlands

The value investor should understand that while Dutch accounting principles frequently simulate US GAAP, although they are perhaps more flexible, some differences do exist. For example, fixed Dutch assets may be stated *in excess* of what was initially paid, that is, the historical cost. Yet only historical cost can be depreciated. Business combinations by and large are treated as purchases, not as poolings of interest.

Goodwill is generally charged against income or retained earnings. Past service costs and pension commitments must be provided for in full. Research and development expenses may be capitalized. Legal reserves are included as part of shareholder equity, not available for dividends. Dutch companies translate earnings of foreign subsidiaries at either the closing exchange rates or average rates while U.S. companies translate earnings of foreign subsidiaries only at average rates.

Japan

Comparing Japanese and American earnings figures or accounting ratios is a futile exercise since most large Japanese companies now publish audited secondary financial statements in English that conform to the U.S. GAAP.

Financial leverage is a way of life in Japan. This doesn't necessarily mean Japanese firms are more risky than their U.S. counterparts, only that banks and their corporate clients have a different relationship.

The most important differences in Japanese accounting principles arise in 12 main areas as shown below. A discussion of the first three then follows:

1. Depreciation.
2. Accounting for intercorporate investments, that is, for subsidiary companies.
3. Inventories.
4. Unfunded pension benefits.
5. Allowance for doubtful accounts.
6. Foreign currency translations.
7. Deferred income taxes.
8. Research and development costs.
9. Installment sales.
10. Stock dividends.
11. Leasing.
12. Specific disclosure.

1.   *Depreciation.*   Just as with issues from The Netherlands or elsewhere, pay close attention to Japanese depreciation. What would happen if the Japanese had to list depreciation the way we do? Then, Japanese earnings would increase some 10 to 13 percent—even more with capital intensive companies.

The reason is that U.S. companies employ mainly straight-line depreciation while the Japanese play a neat trick and use another form called double-declining. (The terminology may be confusing but the idea isn't.)

Straight-line depreciation, perhaps the simplest way to depreciate, runs something like the following:

A machine has a cost of $10,000 and an estimated salvage value of $2,000 at the end of its expected five-year useful life. Depreciation expense for one year is computed thus:

Cost of machinery $10,000
Less: Estimated salvage value   2,000
Depreciable cost $ 8,000

$$\frac{\text{Depreciable cost}}{\text{Estimated life}} = \text{Depreciation expense}$$

$$\frac{\$8,000}{5 \text{ years}} = \$1,600 \text{ per year.}$$

Double-declining-balance speeds things up and provides relatively larger depreciation charges in the early years of an asset's estimated life and gradually decreasing charges later on.

Double-declining-balance for each year is computed by multiplying the asset cost less accumulated depreciation by twice the straight-line rate expressed as a decimal fraction. Using the earlier example—machinery with a cost of $6,000 and a five-year estimated useful life, which is equal to 20 percent per year—depreciation is computed as follows:

First year:	$10,000	×	0.40		$4,000
Second year:	(10,000	−	4,000)	× 0.40	2,400
Third year:	(10,000	−	6,400)	× 0.40	1,440
Fourth year:	(10,000	−	7,840)	× 0.40	864
Fifth year:	(10,000	−	8,704)	× 0.40	518
Total					$9,222

Note that the estimated salvage value is not used directly in these computations, even though the asset retains salvage value. (Since the double-declining-balance procedure will not depreciate the asset to zero cost at the end of the estimated useful life, the residual balance provides an amount in lieu of scrap or salvage value.) What's the difference? Let's compare Ford Motor Company and Honda Motor Company.

In 1987, Ford reported per share earnings of $9.05 per share while Honda's per share earnings almost matched—about $8.54 per share. So far, so good.

Cash flow for the two companies, however, proved vastly different. (As before, cash flow is defined as earnings plus depreciation.) Ford generated $12.69 of cash flow while Honda reported $20.39 per share. Obviously, Honda charged off more to depreciation than Ford did.

What was the net result? Honda's $8.54 per share was effectively more conservative than Ford's $9.05 per share, simply because Honda employs several declining-balance methods of depreciation, including double-declining. As you can see from the example, such procedures provide higher rates.

2. Parent company statements. The investor should carefully note that, for the main, Japanese companies only provide parent company statements, with subsidiaries carried at cost. This again understates earnings. U.S. companies under GAAP include investments and earnings in companies where more than 20 percent is owned.

What does that mean? Since P/E ratios on Japanese stocks are sometimes calculated only on parent company earnings, those earnings would be considerably higher, given the inclusion of subsidiaries' profits. Japanese P/E ratios would be lower under U.S. accounting procedures.

3. Inventory. As with most foreign countries, Japanese inventories are evaluated by FIFO, or first-in, first-out. Be aware that FIFO produces greater reported earnings during periods of inflation.

Japanese companies also have the option of carrying inventory in one of two ways: cost or market. Suppose you owned a fashion garment company with inventories not worth the money put into them. In Japan, such inventories would not be written down but carried at original cost.

U.S. companies, on the other hand, *must* write down the value of inventories if they've dropped below cost.

"Those are all accounting nit picks," a reader might cry. "Completely irrelevant to value investing." Not necessarily.

Australia

Recall if you will the gyrations during 1988 when *The Wall Street Journal's* Linda Sandler reported on Rupert Murdoch's News Corp. News Corp.'s ADRs can be found trading on the NYSE.[1]

Mr. Murdoch's aggressive, debt-financed acquisition program had been well-insulated from the painful effects of costly acquisitions—and their damage to earnings and stock price—by Australia's accounting principles. Under Australian accounting, News Corp.'s ADRs had a P/E ratio of about 8 and you might well have considered them to be a real bargain.

Suppose News Corp. had used U.S. accounting. Its P/E then would have been 17—richer than some less-leveraged publishers. News Corp.'s bankers allowed it to maintain long-term debt—now equivalent to about $4.7 billion—somewhat greater than shareholders' equity. At the time, *Times-Mirror's* debt was equal to 50 percent of equity and the *Washington Post's* was less than 20 percent.

For fiscal 1988, the discrepancy in News Corp.'s earnings under U.S. and Australian accounting was unusually large because it had been excluding operating losses of a subsidiary, Fox Broadcasting, from its results.

A big issue is the value of intangible assets, such as the actual name of a magazine. U.S. companies think twice about such costly acquisitions because they must gradually charge off intangibles against earnings. But News Corp. doesn't have to do that under Australian rules.

Consider. News Corp. finished fiscal 1987 with about $10 billion of assets, about 44 percent of which were intangible. If News Corp. were to use U.S. rules in amortizing intangibles, reported earnings generally would be 25 percent lower.

Periodically, Mr. Murdoch can write up the value of properties, if he thinks they're worth more than he paid. That boosts shareholders' equity—and New Corp.'s borrowing power. In fiscal 1987, asset revaluations totaling $765 million pushed equity to $4 billion. Using Australian rules, News Corp. showed shareholders' equity in 1987 of $4.5 billion; under U.S. accounting the number falls to $2.13 billion.

CURRENCY FLUCTUATIONS

You may have read about currency fluctuations and the part they play in an investor's life. Keep in mind that value investors are long-term players and such fluctuations generally even out over time.

Even so, countries with strong currencies should be avoided because you'll be faced with a strong market—the two seem to go hand-in-hand. When that happens, bargains are few and far between.

Moreover, strong currencies frequently have nowhere else to go but down. That brings not only price vulnerability but also declining prices in terms of the U.S. dollar—all other factors being equal.

Hedging Not Recommended

Foreign exchange risks can be mitigated by foreign exchange hedging. This is done by using either options or futures to lock in a desired exchange rate and thereby protect the return on a stock from the currency fluctuations. For a hedge to be effective, both the amount and time horizon of an investment must be known.

Although, theoretically, foreign exchange hedging is attractive, in practice it proves to be of little use to a value investor. A major problem is the lack of a definite holding period for a foreign equity. An undervalued stock may come to fair value in anywhere from two months to five years.

Additionally, foreign exchange futures and options markets are short-term oriented with the longest available contract usually nine months. The lack of a long-term hedging vehicle and an uncertain holding period make it necessary to roll over short-term positions to be hedged.

Another obstacle is the base size of the futures and option contracts. Each foreign exchange futures contract and option in foreign exchange futures represent on average $80,000, while straight foreign exchange options represent on average $40,000.

Unless an investor has an exposure to a foreign currency of at least these amounts, or, multiples of these amounts, perfect hedges cannot be achieved. Based on these arguments, an imperfect hedge which is no longer riskless is the best that can be hoped for.

Finally, foreign currency hedging is not cheap. The premium on a contract can run from 2 percent to 7 percent. Rolling over a position every three months for five years could cost you from 35 percent to 75 percent of your original investment. A stock would have to do incredibly well to overcome that drain on return.

Hedging to insulate a stock from the effects of foreign exchange movements becomes nothing more than a costly gamble—something that has no place in a rational approach to value investments.

Value stocks are generally found in countries where the economy, currency, and stock market have not been doing well. Therefore, you automatically avoid high priced currencies that are due for a fall. Also, for a long-term investor, currency fluctuations will tend to even out. It is for these reasons that I do not recommend currency hedging.

Let's turn now to some other overseas complexities.

CHARACTERISTICS OF
OVERSEAS MARKETS

Mastering the idiosyncrasies of some foreign markets can be worthwhile for the direct or ADR investor; other markets should be avoided under any circumstances.

Some markets handicap nonresident investors, placing premiums on certain stocks, withholding voting rights, or even going so far as to limit the number of shares which can be owned or to place some issues off limits for direct trading.

For instance, the Swiss pharmaceutical house, Ciba-Geigy, whose shares could be purchased by Swiss investors for 1,300 Swiss francs in 1988, charged outsiders double that rate at 2,600 Swiss francs.

Stay away from "flea market" exchanges that operate as private clubs. Arab stock markets are not to be recommended partly because the Islamic legal code allows debtors to walk away. In general, watch for relatively lax standards concerning insider status. Foreign countries have loose disclosure requirements.

On the bright side, foreign exchanges are becoming better organized with more safeguards and more assistance. Just find out the rules before getting involved.

EMERGING MARKETS

Perhaps the best approach to emerging markets is through a specialized fund like the ones presented in Chapter 10. Even so, emerging markets (EMs) have come of age. So let's briefly address them.

EXHIBIT 10–2
Market Capitalization, Turnover, and Number of Listings

	Market Capitalization* Billions of US$		Turnover Ratio*,†		Number of Listings
	1980	1984	1980	1983	1984
Emerging Markets					
Argentina	4.0	1.2	29	13	236
Brazil	20.0	28.9	21	25	608
Chile	10.3	2.1	16	2	220
India	6.0	7.9	44	62	3882
Jordan	1.6	2.2	9	12	131
Korea	3.8	6.1	49	50	336
Mexico	13.0	2.8	18	37	178
Thailand	1.2	1.7	26	20	89
Zimbabwe	1.8	0.2	11	20	56
Developed Markets					
United States	1347.5	1788.5	31	45	6330
Japan (Tokyo only)	379.2	644.4	44	50	1444
United Kingdom	205.2	242.7	19	18	2171
Germany	71.7	78.4	21	37	449
France (Paris only)	54.6	41.1	26	30	504
Belgium	10.0	12.2	21	29	197
Denmark (Copenhagen only)	5.5	7.6	1	2‡	236
Norway (Oslo only)	3.2	5.8	3	38‡	148
Finland (Helsinki only)	N.A.	4.2	N.A.	10‡	52
Austria (Vienna only)	2.0	1.5	5	8‡	100

* In some instances, both market capitalization and turnover ratio are for only the major exchange in the particular EM, thereby understating the actual figures.
† Turnover ratio is annual trading volume as a percentage of market capitalization.
‡ 1984 data

Source: International Finance Corporation, Washington, D.C.

First, the tendency by investors to lump EMs together as a homogeneous group is a mistake and a way to cut down excellent opportunities. The fact is that some EMs are at least as attractive as smaller markets in already developed economies. (See Exhibit 10–2.) Many emulate U.S. and U.K. financial regulations.

Several researchers, including Levy, Sarnat, Errunz, and Rosenberg, have found EMs relatively less risky than developed markets, particularly for large corporate investors.[2] International investors can better bear liquidity and diversification constraints of individual firms and markets than can domestic investors who primarily hold local assets.

CONCLUSION

Chapters 9 and 10 have armed you with significant fundamentals regarding overseas value investing.

The following chapters address the way to put these fundamental concepts to work. The goal is to assist you in building and preserving wealth over the lifetime of an investment. Unlike the pitch of the TV huckster and some financial writers, the cry is not, "Hurry, hurry, hurry." Instead, as I have noted previously, the value investing philosophy is a patient approach.

NOTES

1. Linda Sandler, "Heard On The Street," *The Wall Street Journal,* August 16, 1988. Reprinted by permission of *The Wall Street Journal,* © Dow Jones & Company, Inc. (1988). All Rights Reserved Worldwide.
2. Vihang Errunz and Etienne Losq, "How Risky Are Emerging Markets?," *Journal of Portfolio Management,* Fall 1987, p. 62.

CHAPTER 11

HOW TO PLAN
YOUR INVESTING

So far, just the background music has been provided. Basic facts and fundamentals have been given in detail on how to invest on both domestic and global scales with value methods. Rules have been given throughout the preceding pages that should improve an investor's productivity and provide greater success.

Even so, background music isn't enough. A correctly developed investment plan is an important—no, vital—cornerstone of successful value investing. The second cornerstone is to follow that plan.

Chapter 11 addresses a method by which the average investor can determine how to allocate investable funds. The chapter also highlights key elements, some guidelines, and a few rules.

Next, Chapter 12 examines several practical aspects; in other words, how to piece together and operate various elements that spring naturally from a value investing plan.

DEFINITION OF AN INVESTMENT PLAN

Sometimes it's easier to define something by saying what it isn't An investment plan isn't anything as simplistic as the hoary foolproof saying: "Buy low and sell high." As an investor, it does mean to formalize—in writing—an asset mix that contains *your* personal insight and *your* knowledge of the investment world.

The next linked step is to systematically and tenaciously acquire value assets, based upon that plan, through market cycle after market cycle.

WHY AN INVESTMENT PLAN?

The reader may wonder why an investment plan is necessary. It is to protect ourselves from ourselves.

Creating a well-defined investment plan equips the average investor with a powerful and effective focus and helps to diffuse the noise and cacophony of options and alternatives. Moreover, a plan gives an investor the wherewithal to stick to it—no matter what else is happening.

No one likes to think of making financial decisions while running on their emotional cylinders. But think back to the October 1987 decline and consider—as an investor and not a speculator.

The average investor clearly profits most when purchasing shares at lower prices, simply because more shares can be purchased with the same amount of money and more returns can be generated. Conversely, you, as an investor, should only desire higher stock prices if selling. (Selling here doesn't mean the game of market timing but a final, permanent, liquidation.) Yet, many investors grow anxious when prices decline. Instead of seeing the wonderful opportunities depressed markets create for long-term investors, they freeze or, worse, panic. By the same token, they grow elated when prices soar.

The conclusion is apparent. An unambiguous, long-term investment plan offers protection against "instant fixes" at times of crisis or elation. Such plans tend to cull out dangerous emotions, organize thinking, and permit judgments to be made based upon internal and external factors.

How to Go about It

The formation of an investment plan is not all that complex. Constructing one mainly calls for the investment of a small amount of time and a modicum of sound thought and consideration. But these ingredients *are* vital and can be effectively added only by the investor.

Why? Because only the investor can speak with relevance and credibility to an overall financial and investment situation. By that is meant the earning power and ability to save, plus any tolerance for changes in market prices, particularly when pressures and stresses mount.

Additionally, the investor should be aware of the proper target on which the investment plan should be focussed. The target is not long-term common stock *results:* these are not the focus of an investment plan.

What is critical is *whether a properly diversified portfolio* can be selected, with stocks purchased at reasonable prices, and *the program continued* through fluctuations that are the normal nature of equity investing.

Six Questions to Guide Your Thinking

Now let's turn to several guidelines. The average investor could put the following six key questions to good use while preparing an investment plan.

1. What are your financial resources? This is the obvious first step: To analyze your situation and determine how much you can set aside for investment purposes.

2. How important is your portfolio to your overall financial position? Large pension funds can usually take greater short-term market risks than can retired widows who are dependent upon income from investments and who need a certain fixed yield.

If your situation permits, it makes more sense to invest for maximum total long-term returns and withdraw small amounts from capital than to limit returns so that high current dividends are received.

3. What are the real risks involved with your short-run plans? Long-run plans? Might you need working capital for your business in a recessionary period—at the same time equity prices might be low? Do you have a set of triplets entering Stanford in two years? Have sufficient funds been set aside to cover the "basics"? Does your promotion to company president hinge upon how the pension fund performs over the next year?

How many years ahead are you looking for the major benefits of your investments? Suppose you're 35 years old and have all of your obligations under control. In that case you can look 10 or 20 years ahead and buy certain companies. On the other hand, if you're 80 and you need a certain amount of current income from limited means, the strategy will be different.

4. What would the consequences be of unanticipated interim fluctuations? Pension funds, for example, could be forced to augment contributions if the market value of their portfolios drops below a preset triggering level.

5. How knowledgeable about investments and markets are you? It's not necessary to be a security analyst. Even so, the average investor should have a firm grasp on basic principles. Unknowledgeable investors frequently grow timid during bear markets and brash beyond all measure during bull markets. Both ways are costly.

6. What are your probable emotional reactions to the market as well as to adverse experience? A "Woody Allen" type investor shouldn't attempt to adopt the role of Indiana Jones. Some investors care about eating well, others about sleeping well. Whichever category fits, stay well within prescribed tolerance levels for interim fluctuations. That includes differing time frames such as quarter-to-quarter fluctuations or bull-to-bear market fluctuations. It's one thing to go through short-term changes, it's quite another to absorb and accept full bear markets. By determining a pain threshold as well as investment staying power the investor has the basis for determining acceptable equity levels.

Can manufactured "crises" be dismissed, particularly those coming from brokers who wish the investor to switch holdings under short-term thinking? Will the investor consider short-term quotational losses as wonderful opportunities or become emotionally paralyzed into inaction or galvanized into inappropriate selling, resolving never to buy equities again? Will you recognize that when prices reach their lows, pessimism by definition has to be close to its nadir?

Add to Your Check List

As a value investor, you might add the answers to the following questions. What is your family situation? What are the ages, health, and number of the prime beneficiaries? What is your occupation and the amount of income expected from the occupation? Your tax bracket? Income from other sources? How much debt do you have and when is its maturity? What potential benefits do you have under estates, trusts, or retirement plans?

Critical examination of each of the above concerns can be vitally important. The investor must dig carefully into those areas before a logically tailored and selective plan can be defined.

Comparing Results

Don't compare apples and oranges and don't compare value and growth portfolios—at least, over the short term. In the long run, it's perhaps better to judge a portfolio's *performance* only in relation to its philosophy and plan and the results that should be obtained.

Take, for example, a value portfolio (the philosophy) with a maximum commitment to equities of 75 percent of investable funds (the plan). Here, the question that might be asked, would be: was the return reasonable considering the level of risk assumed?

Here is yet another yardstick: The performance of an equity portfolio should be based on total assets committed and not just the securities' portion. In other words, the reserves of cash that have been set aside for investing purposes should be counted in, not counted out, in measuring performance.

A word of warning. Measuring performance tends to be counterproductive. In most instances, it tends to redirect thinking toward short-term results. That's not what the average value investor focuses on.

Instead, performance measurement should establish whether a portfolio is being managed along preset guidelines, particularly as to market risk and type of security.

Time Is Important

So far we've emphasized the importance of long-term thinking. Here are several other tips that should prove to be important in assembling a portfolio.

Next to proper stock selection, *the length of time an investment is held can be the most important element in an investment program.*

The true investor will search for investments that offer the highest potential returns. These returns might only be realized long term and could lose money over the short term.

Time can transform investments from undesirable to attractive for one simple reason: *Average expected rates* of return are not at all affected by time but the *range or distribution of actual returns around the expected average are.*

Charles Ellis, in his book *Investment Policy,* demonstrates this point in a deliberately highly exaggerated but quite relevant example.[1] To show the importance of time, Mr. Ellis uses returns to be expected on a one-day investment in a common stock. Mr. Ellis notes:

> The typical stock's share price is $40, and the range of trading during the day might easily be from 39¼ to 40½—a range of 1¼ or 3.1 percent of the average price for the day. Remembering that in today's market, with today's expectations for future inflation, the average annual rate of return for common stocks is approximately 15 percent, let's postulate that an investment in this hypothetical stock would have an expected daily return of 0.06 percent (15 percent annual return divided into 250 trading days) and a range around that expected average of plus or minus 1.55 percent (3.1 percent intraday range divided by two).
>
> Now, let's annualize that daily return of 0.06 percent and that 3.1 percent daily variation. The average annual expected rate of return would be 15 percent, but the range of returns around the 15 percent would be a daunting plus or minus 387.5 percent. In other words, the annual rate of return for a one-day investment in our hypothetical stock would be somewhere between a profit of 405.5 percent and a loss of 372.5 percent.

In real life the above example would be highly unlikely. Clearly those time frames are too short for equities since the expected variation in return is too great compared with the average expected return. In other words, they're simply speculations on price changes.

Time also helps the investor determine risk/reward tradeoffs—not an easy task. In fact, many investors, including institutional pro's, currently have lost sight of the time concept. Goaded by fear of short-term price fluctuations, this group has invested less in equities than appropriate under long-run thinking.[2] The result has been to sacrifice much in the way of gains in an effort to achieve stability.

CONCLUSION

The formation of a philosophy and a plan to implement such an investment program is vital for long-term investment success.

Individual investors must draw up their own plans. This cannot be delegated for several reasons.

Responsible and knowledgeable third parties tend to be conservative and conventional since they usually have nothing to gain if the investment program is successful but plenty to lose (legally and otherwise) given short-term problems. Moreover, third parties are unlikely to address the potential returns lost by avoiding long-term investing in equities. (Naturally, they can provide guidance and background information.)

In Chapter 11 we presented arguments in favor of formulating an investment plan and philosophy. Addressed also were six key questions to serve as guidelines during the making of the plan. The importance of investment time horizons and the proper application of performance measurements were also discussed.

Now let's turn to Chapter 12 and the practical aspects of operating a value portfolio.

NOTES

1. Charles D. Ellis, *Investment Policy* (Homewood, IL: Dow Jones-Irwin, 1985), pp. 30–31.

2. Time horizons usually run something like this (considering the leveling effect of time): a 5-year horizon uses a 60:40 ratio of equities to bonds; a 10-year horizon uses an 80:20 ratio; and a 15-year horizon should result in a 90:10 ratio, and so forth. Such time horizons would be incorrect for institutions charged with a long-term (30 years or more) investment horizon. Yet typically pension funds during the late 1970s and early 1980s placed only 50 percent of their funds in equities and geared more to three- or four-year time horizons. The result has been for them to lose opportunities for greater returns. Frequently, too, no difference seems to exist between asset mixes of such obviously disparate categories as employee benefit plans and endowment funds or companies with old work forces and those with young ones.

CHAPTER 12

STRUCTURING YOUR VALUE PORTFOLIO

Superb value portfolios just don't happen. They start with a plan centered in the mind of an investor and are tailored to specific needs and requirements. These needs and requirements are derived from the answers to several key questions outlined in the preceding chapter.

In Chapter 12 we consider the concept of risk as it applies to value investing and then explore both diversification and the idea of *effective* diversification as a way to minimize risk. Arguments are then presented in favor of an all-stock portfolio, with empirical evidence used to bolster this theory. Since performance measurement plays an important role for any investor it's touched on again from a different angle than in the preceding chapter. Reasons why the concepts of liquidity and dollar averaging do not play important roles for value investors are emphasized. Last, since value investors will not always be fully invested, several financial mechanisms have been suggested as places to park investable funds.

RISK—APPLIED TO VALUE INVESTING

The value investor would find the traditional Wall Street definition of risk—investment risk depends on share price fluctuations—to be unacceptable. Value investors simply don't lose money merely because share prices decline—even if they temporarily drop under buyer cost.

Risk, for the average value investor, can more relevantly be defined as the product of one of three events: loss realized through actual sale; significant deterioration in a company's position; or, more frequently, payment of more than the intrinsic worth of the security.

NOTHING LIKE DIVERSIFICATION

Even in a correctly structured value portfolio risk exists, and, as a result, diversification plays a strong role. Even with value stocks, nuggets of gold may turn out to be "fool's gold."

Purchasing only one value issue, or investing in only one industry, suggests that choice will perform better than all others. That, in itself, is a gamble and, while it may prove correct, the average investor is taking an unnecessary risk.

Diversification, not putting all your eggs in one basket, can save you a good deal of Excedrin. The example in Exhibit 12–1 illustrates the beneficial impact of diversification. Notice how risk plummets far and fast when the number of stocks in a portfolio are increased to a minimum of 20.

EXHIBIT 12–1

Number of Issues in Portfolio	Percent of Total Risk	Percent by Which Risk Reduced	Cumulative Risk Reduction
1	100%	0%	0%
2	80	20	20
3	75	5	25
4	70	5	30
5	65	5	35
6	60	5	40
7	58	2	42
8	56	2	44
9	54	2	46
10	52	2	48
15	47	5	53
20	45%	2%	55%

Source: Peter D. Heerwagen, *Investing for Total Return* (Chicago: Probus, 1988). pg. 32.

Should a value investor then consider 20 stocks to be the limit, a cutoff point, so to speak? Not really. The Tweedy Brown portfolio, highlighted in Chapter 1, includes some 300 different value stocks. In fact, there is no maximum cutoff point. The point that a value investor should keep in mind is this:

returns are not diluted by an increased number of portfolio issues—so long as strict value criteria are followed.

Getting the Right Slant on Diversification

Graham's arguments over diversification favored investors dividing funds between high-grade bonds and high-grade common stocks.[1] Many of today's professional investors concur in varying degrees with Graham's argument, although my belief differs. Times and conditions have changed. Graham's rule was simple, mechanistic, and, perhaps not appropriate for the current investing world.

Somewhat Different Today
Given today's investing climate, value investors should consider placing their emphasis on equities to the total exclusion of preferred stocks or bonds. In other words, the average value investor ideally should place 100 percent of total investable funds in diversified equities that trade at 60 percent of intrinsic value.

A somewhat heretical philosophy, to be certain. But if skepticism over its soundness exists, a simple scan of the Ibbotson chart illustrated in the next chapter provides food for thought. Notice that stocks *always* outperform bonds *over the long term*.

Or, consider the merits of an all-stock portfolio provided by a recent study conducted by Meir Statman and Neal L. Ushman at Santa Clara University, Santa Clara, California.

Based upon data gathered from 1946 to 1985, the two researchers discovered that during the 40-year postwar period a portfolio of *only stocks* was better than either a *market portfolio* or a *strictly bond* portfolio[2].

To be sure, full investment may not always be possible. A

EXHIBIT 12–2
Portfolios over the 1946–1985 Period

	Mean Quarterly Excess Return	Standard Deviation of Excess Return
Stocks only	1.834	7.543
Corporate bonds only	0.060	4.653
Market Portfolio	−0.102	4.548

full complement of bargain issues occurs only about every four or five years. Moreover, it usually takes three years from the time value buys are available until sales become significant. Practically, however, value investors can find enough issues to be at least 25 percent invested, especially if horizons have been broadened to include global issues.

When Should Stocks Be Purchased?

When things can be found that are cheap enough to buy, the time is ripe to buy.

When prices are so high that nothing can be found at appropriate prices, the market is too high—don't buy.

During 1970, 1974, and 1981 vast numbers of value stocks were available; it was obvious the market was low. But, remember that the average value investor is not buying "the market" but selected businesses. As such, the value investor invests according to how the market *is,* not where it *will* be.

EFFECTIVE DIVERSIFICATION

Thus far the discussion has centered around an investor's portfolio mix and the number of stocks to be included. That's *diversification.* The focus can now be narrowed somewhat to *effective diversification.*

Unpopular issues and, therefore, bargain prices tend to fall into terms of industries. So the investor discovering a value stock located in one particular industry should avoid next-door-neighbor stocks within the same industry. One good rule of thumb to follow: no more than 20 percent of an investor's portfolio should come from one industry.

For example, a portfolio of 10 consumer electronics stocks would not be effective diversification—even if all were value stocks. Certainly, although each has some unique characteristics and influences, strong group influences exist that would tend to move them at the same time. Effective diversification requires stocks to be independent of each other.

An industry's basic economics may change. Keep in mind the poor horse and buggy dealers when the automobile zoomed along.

Full Scientific Approach Unnecessary

A fully scientific approach to diversification requires an enormous amount of number crunching and many long hours sorting out the relationships between stocks and stock groups. There are investment professionals who do just that, wringing out the last drop of risk reduction.

Value investors need mainly to use a little common sense to decide on an appropriate number of stocks, and then to spread them over a broad spectrum of dissimilar industries.

Diversification Not Free

Naturally diversification costs more—in terms of commissions, spreads, and taxes. Commissions on 200 shares each of two stocks, for example, cost more than for 400 shares of one stock. But, by not diversifying, the investor has placed an inappropriate reliance on skill or luck to determine investment results.

Factors Considered in Measuring Performance

Imagine that as an investor you've selected and purchased value securities and now have a portfolio. The next question may well be "how is performance measured?"

Certainly not by short-run results. These should be taken

with several grains of salt—if not completely ignored. The plain truth is that short-run performances report randomly generated numbers—only a snapshot of prices as opposed to a time exposure.

The following should be chiseled in concrete: *don't attempt to gauge results until a portfolio has turned over at least once.* (That could happen once every three to five years.)

The short- or intermediate-term concern of the average value investor should be addressed to whether current operations match philosophy and established plan. If they don't, then it becomes irrelevant as to whether results are plus or minus. The truly important feedback is that the portfolio is haphazard and sailing along without a well-defined plan. Sooner or later, that means a financial shipwreck. Of course, other practical lessons also surface.

First, stock and/or group risk estimates are at best only problematical and based mainly on past behavior. Moreover, relationships frequently change between the market's reaction and a specific stock or portfolio. So even past performances are not reliable indicators of future movement.

Second, one skillful and/or lucky decision can make or break a portfolio. How would returns have appeared with Genentech tucked snugly away from inception? What are the chances of finding another?

Or, consider the incredibly large returns received by a well-diversified partnership after it purchased 50 percent of the equity of one business. Prior to the purchase, the partnership had performed well—20 percent annually—by acquiring hundreds of value stocks.

Describing it, Benjamin Graham related, "ironically enough, the aggregate of profits accruing from this single investment decision far exceeded the sum of all others realized through 20 years of wide ranging operations. . . ." Although disguised by Graham, the partnership was the Graham-Newman Corporation; the company was GEICO Insurance[3].

Consider, too, performance numbers can vary enormously depending on starting and ending dates. Superb performances become quite ordinary, and vice versa, simply by adding or subtracting one year.

LIQUIDITY

Wall Street attention focuses largely on a stock's liquidity, the extent to which a market absorbs purchases or sales without large price changes. Wall Street sticks like sandpaper to liquid issues, so that if word goes around, a fast retreat can be made.

Again, worrying about liquidity problems simply wastes the time and limits the opportunities of value investors. Value investors invest long term—not buying and selling on a dime, day by day. The following case illustrates that notion.

A Case in Point: Delaware Trust Company

Delaware Trust Company, a small bank, was one of a score of companies that Wall Street consistently overlooked; perhaps because the story wasn't sexy enough or perhaps because its float was too thin. Whatever the reason, Delaware was not bathed in the financial-community limelight; investors and institutions stayed away from it.

Yet, it was packed with profit potential. The book value for Delaware was over $120 per share and the stock, priced at $45 when it traded—was pegged at four times earnings.

I learned more about the company, then sent away for shareholder information, which definitely heightened my interest on its arrival. Enough so, that in 1978, I acquired a position in Delaware, obtaining a few hundred shares of stock over a six-month period. Delaware traded "by appointment only," sometimes not trading for three months at a time. Every six months the bank's business activities were reviewed. Note from the accompanying table that for the first two or three years very little progress was made but, in 1984, the stock began to move dramatically.

Delaware was finally purchased in 1987 by the Meridien Bank which paid shareholders $853 per share. In my case, that amount translated into a 33 percent per year compounded rate of return. Yet Delaware's stock was non-liquid. Liquidity is not important for long-term value investors. It is important only for short-term speculators.

EXHIBIT 12–3
History Of A Value Purchase

As of end of February	Value of 82 shares
1979	$ 4,600
1980	5,002
1981	5,412
1982	6,437
1983	7,544
1984	10,455
1985	16,400
1986	21,320
1987	38,950
1987 (May)	$70,000*

* Buyout
Relevant statistics:
   On September 8, 1978, 82 shares of Delaware Trust Co. were purchased for one account for $4,600. A medium-sized full service bank, Delaware had $500 million in total assets in 1978. Its P/E was 4.35; price to book value, 35 percent; return on equity, 8 percent; return on assets .5 percent; and actual loan loss, .15 percent.

Dollar Averaging

Dollar averaging proponents believe that as long as an investor can take advantage of fluctuations, buying more stock when prices fall and less when prices rise, on balance the investor will come out all right.

Dollar averagers, in other words, say they don't know what price to pay for something. Perhaps money can be made in this way, but that doesn't qualify as value investing.

Value investors only buy when the price gets to where it's a bargain. And the prudent value investor knows that spot before the pocketbook has been initially opened and will not purchase stock at any price higher than that. Naturally, an investor would increase a position if the stock declined in price. Value investors don't sell just because the price declines, assuming the business fundamentals remain the same. Just the opposite. We'd be interested in purchasing more of the stock.

Places to Put Noninvested Cash

Suppose an investor has a pocketful of cash and hasn't encountered a suitable value stock? The prudent investor should attempt to keep all investable funds liquid in case a bargain suddenly appears. One good place to do so would be in highly liquid, short-term instruments. Several appropriate financial mechanisms have been listed below.

MONEY MARKET FUNDS

One of the bigger players on the field would be money market funds. Money market funds pool assets and invest them in short-term money market instruments, taking a small percentage of the total portfolio yield as a service charge and then returning the rest to the individual investor in proportion to the amount of money he has invested.

Of the hundreds of money market funds available, some two dozen invest strictly in government securities. Other portfolios are divided into commercial paper, short-term repurchase agreements (usually governmental), CDs, foreign CDs, bankers' acceptances (used to finance foreign trade), federal agency securities, and U.S. Treasury bills.

Money markets have varying yields. With demands persisting for credit from corporations and the government alike, money market fund yields ranged between 6 percent and 8 percent throughout 1987 and into 1988.

Treasury Bills and Notes

There are scores of different government issues, carrying different coupon rates and different maturities.

Treasury bills are short-term obligations, issued with initial maturities of three, six, and twelve months, and sold in minimum amounts of $10,000 with additional increments of $5,000. They come with initial maturities of 3, 6, and 12 months. A new batch of three- and six-month T-bills is auctioned publicly every Monday, while new issues of one-year bills are sold every month.

Ownership is signified by a Treasury book entry rather than through the more familiar engraved certificate. Prices of new bills are set by competitive investor bidding following an offering announcement.

Ask your broker or bank to handle the details of the transaction. There will be a small commission fee.

Treasury notes are like T-bills but mature instead in 1 to 10 years from the date of issue. Although the minimum denomination for notes is $1,000, the Treasury sometimes sets higher minimums for particular issues. Keep in mind that T-bills and T-notes are not state taxable whereas with all other cash instruments you're doubly taxed.

Certificates of Deposits (CDs)

CDs can prove attractive—as long as funds are not tied up too long and bargain stock issues are missed. CD rates can be higher than either T-bills or money market funds. The staggering of maturities permits an investor some liquidity in case a bargain issue pops up. Otherwise, the investor would be whacked by a penalty on the interest rate normally received.

Commercial Paper

Another possibility, particularly for large investors, would be commercial paper. Commercial paper, usually sold in lots of $100,000, can be purchased for maturities that range from overnight to 30 or 180 days and even a year or longer. Current yields are slightly higher than comparable maturities of T-bills and T-notes. Commercial paper can be purchased directly from General Motors in Detroit in minimums of $10,000.

Tax Exempt Municipal Bonds

Finally—if a tax bracket justifies it—consider short term tax exempt municipal bonds.

CONCLUSION

The preceding pages have addressed risk and why diversification plays an important role. They have also provided several key tips for effective diversification. Also presented was the belief that, while it runs contrary to Wall Street thinking, solid evidence exists for assembling an all-equity value portfolio. Traditionally, fundamental investor wisdom invokes the merits of liquidity and dollar averaging. The chapter presents salient reasons why such methods do not play significant roles for the value investor.

One additional observation. Learning to sit quietly and do nothing is probably the greatest lesson a value investor can learn. An investor should not assume that because cash is on hand it must be invested.

The next logical question is really a basic one: Why should you invest in common stocks at all? That answer comes in Chapter 13.

NOTES

1. Graham favored an investor dividing funds between high-grade bonds and high-grade common stocks. The correct proportion, his argument ran, would be no less than 25 percent or more than 75 percent of funds in common stocks. A corollary to that called for an inverse range of between 75 percent and 25 percent of funds placed in bonds. The implication was a 50/50 split between the two major investment mediums. Following that theory, if changes in market level raised the common stock component to 55 percent the investor would simply sell one-eleventh of a stock component and put the proceeds into bonds. And vice-versa. Times and conditions have changed. Graham's thoughts centered around late 1971 and early 1972, a period when bond yields more than doubled stock yields. Moreover, he addressed himself to all of an investor's investable funds—the portion allocated for bonds or stocks.

   He also dismissed the effects of time horizons rather casually and failed to show the long haul advantages that equities enjoy over bonds.

2. Meir Statman and Neal L. Ushman, "Bonds versus stocks: Another look", *Journal of Portfolio Management,* Winter, 1987, pp. 33–38.
3. Benjamin Graham, *The Intelligent Investor* (New York: Harper & Row), 1973, Postscript.

CHAPTER 13

ARE STOCKS A GOOD INVESTMENT?

Our economic system faces new and difficult problems, yet I remain optimistic. Perhaps I haven't made that clear, so let me take a moment to emphasize that point.

Industrial economies in the past have survived and even flourished under far greater economic pressures than those now being experienced. Real estate, bonds, and other assets can maintain their value only within a viable economic system. Businesses generate the wealth that fuels that system. Many investors lose sight of the fact that values are interrelated. If businesses falter, many other areas will be affected.

Clearly capital has sought wildly for a safe haven during this decade. Clearly, too, the usually prudent methods of capital preservation—bank deposits, bonds, and mortgages—may lead to a melting away of purchasing power. Faced with weakening confidence, puzzling inflation, and greater economic concern, people have flooded alternative markets like art, coins, real estate, commodities, and bonds. Without question, those alternatives have a place in investment portfolios.

Even so, Chapter13 presents arguments in favor of equities as an *investment*—a long haul commitment—along with insights into market ups and downs, including bear markets. Comparisons are made between equities and other financial alternatives. Again, the effect of time is touched upon as is the challenge of inflation.

STOCKS AS AN INVESTMENT

Are stocks a good investment? The reader can be the judge. Exhibit 13–1 outlines two sets of performance figures.

The first set includes performance figures that have been compiled for various market indicators over 1987 and also for the past 62 years. All of the numbers are as of December 31, 1987.

Cash, measured by T-bills, obviously proved somewhat better during 1987 than stocks. During the past 62 years, however, including 1987, stocks have more effectively built wealth.

Perhaps the reader might give consideration to a 1983 study, one that measured Graham's stock selection criteria over a period that ranged from 1974 to 1981.[1]

Here a control group of NYSE-AMEX securities provided a mean annual return (including dividends) of 14 percent. An investor who used Graham's criteria and the same stock selection universe would have been presented with an annual return of 38 percent. Furthermore, excess returns remained after risk adjustment and adjustment for firm size effects.

A second 13-year study, which included the early 1980s, used essentially the same criteria. Again the value portfolio considerably outperformed the control portfolio of NYSE-AMEX and small firm indexes.[2]

For example, an investor that had placed $10,000 in a Graham-oriented portfolio on December 31, 1970, would have seen that increase to $254,973 by year end 1983. The com-

EXHIBIT 13–1
Comparison of Stocks, Bonds, and T-bills

Index	1987	1925-87
S & P 500	5.3%	9.85%*
T-bills	6.1	3.51
Corporate bonds	10.7	5.00

* Dividends reinvested

parable figures for the NYSE-AMEX and small firm indexes would have been $37,296 and $101,992, respectively.

What about Bear Markets?

Consider that since World War II ended 10 bear markets have been formed. Each lasted an average of 12 months and experienced an average 26 percent drop in the Dow-Jones Industrial Average (see Exhibit 13–2). The average rise during the first year that followed each of the 10 market declines approximated 38 percent.

Compare Stocks with Other Assets

How do common stocks stack up compared with antiques, bonds, Treasuries, gold, and copper? See Exhibit 13–3 where the 1975 to 1985 period has been clearly depicted.

Notice from the chart that stocks have outperformed bonds and T-bills. That's no surprise. "Exhibit 13–3 is skewed," some readers might complain. "The comparison started early in 1975 at the beginning of a major bull market."

Those readers would be right. On the other hand, the test ended at a bad time for stocks—1984. What if 1986 figures had been used? Stocks would have left the others in the backstretch regardless of when the analysis began. Stocks have performed

EXHIBIT 13–2

Bear Market	Life Span (months)	Price Decline	First Year Rise after Decline
1948–49	8	−15.7%	42.7%
1953	8	−13.8	42.9
1957	3	−20.4	32.1
1960	10	−18.0	30.0
1961–62	7	−29.2	39.7
1966	8	−26.5	29.3
1968–70	18	−36.9	52.7
1973–74	21	−46.3	42.4
1976–78	17	−28.2	11.1
1981–82	16	−25.1	53.6

better than fixed-income alternatives for decades. Notice the comparison, however, with hard money alternatives.

GOLD

Take gold. Unless an investor had sold gold at the top, only 4.8 percent would have been earned on an annualized basis. That's less than returns brandished by your friendly neighborhood bank. Nor would long-term holding have given better results. From 1781 to 1981, gold went up only 1.6% annually. (In 1980 the reader would have received 1.9 percent.) How about 1926 to 1981? That was gold's glittering period. During this time gold shot up 5.8 percent per year, nicely beating both inflation and returns on short-term T-bills.

EXHIBIT 13–3
Stock versus Five Investment Alternatives, 1975 to 1985

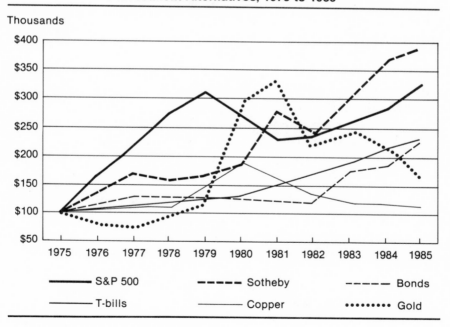

Source: *Forbes*, March 11, 1985 p. 222.

All activity in gold, however, occurred over 10 years. Look even closer. In 4 of every 5 years, you would have been left standing at the gate. Some inflation hedge. A buy-and-hold strategy with a diversified group of stocks would have served much better.

COMMODITIES

Not surprisingly, many investors pick commodities as their road to instant wealth. Perhaps it is useful to examine commodities—the fastest game in town. Commodities give even professionals—armed with sophisticated trading techniques and spanking new computers—fits.

Money magazine recently observed that 90 percent of small investors lost both their money and their taste for commodities within four months. Small wonder. Given the speed, volatility, leverage, and pressure inherent in the commodities business, four months could well seem like 10 years.

FINE ART

Fine art has been the one hard-money asset that gives stocks a run for their money—going up more than 12.5 percent annually.

But the difficulties may outweigh the good points. Today's "in" painting may prove difficult to sell tomorrow and transaction costs could be sizeable. Stocks have the advantage of being able to be sold quickly, with commissions running less than 1 percent through a discount broker.

REAL ESTATE

Real estate and inflation have been closely linked for most Americans—but it's also a way to get trapped. Unleveraged real estate has proven to be a mediocre long-term investment, barely keeping up with inflation. See Exhibit 13–4.

Compare real estate's return over the long haul with those stocks have produced. The reader can see that raw land offers

EXHIBIT 13–4

**Cumulative Wealth Indexes of Capital Market Security Groups,
1947–1984 (year-end 1946 = $1)**

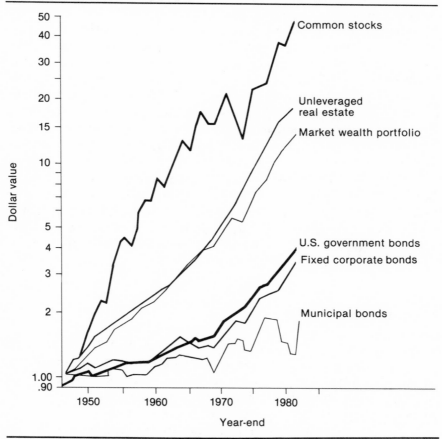

Source: Roger G. Ibbotson and Laurence B. Siegel, "Real Estate Returns: A Comparison with Other Investments," *AREUEA Journal*, vol. 12, no. 3, Fall 1984, p. 225.

even worse returns. Home price appreciation proves better, but again, not superior, to stocks.

Unlike businesses, real estate does not produce or create wealth at all. The value of real estate is based upon what rents can be achieved and on how well business does. Single-family home costs have to be paid by people making enough to cover them. So businesses have to be more profitable than real estate or real estate rents cannot be paid and houses cannot be purchased.

Why does everyone believe real estate is so profitable? One word—leveraging—that is, the use of borrowed money. Most real estate profits have stemmed from leveraging to the eyeballs, particularly when real estate prices are rising. The downside, of course, is that while paper profits go up by borrowing so do potential losses. Many investors have forgotten that risk exists in real estate, thanks to the persistence of an inflation that has pervaded the economy over the past few decades.

Take Texas real estate. All of the major banks in the state have gone under at this time due mainly to real estate and oil loans. If businesses don't do well, neither does real estate. If the banks lose their shirts on mortgage loans, obviously the equity owners will do worse. Leverage will have wiped out 100 percent of their investments in real estate.

STOCKS OR BONDS

Which is better, stocks or bonds? Consider Exhibit 13–5 from Ibbotson Associates, for the answer. Exhibit 13–5 measures rates of return provided by classes of securities. This study, together with the well-known Fisher/Lorie one, has proved that stocks perform better than the other investments.

The study, initiated in 1926, eliminates temporary distortions caused by the Great Depression. Suppose $1 had been invested in common stocks at year-end 1925. Including appreciations and dividends, that dollar would have grown to $347.96 by year-end 1987—a 9.9 percent annual rate of return. Suppose $1 was invested in small company stocks over the same period. The dollar investment would then have grown to $1,202.97.

Obviously, such returns far outdistance the 4 percent average annual inflation rate. (Notice that returns generated by T-bills and long-term government bonds just matched inflation.)

Researchers also have discovered a phenomenal 12.1 percent average annual return from so-called small stocks. Now

EXHIBIT 13–5

Wealth Indices of Investments in U.S. Capital Markets, 1926–1987 (year-end 1925 = 1.00)

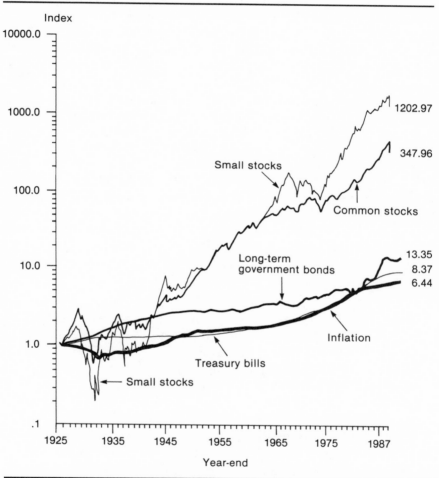

well-documented, the phenomena is called the "small-firm effect." Why are long-term rates of return on stocks better than bonds and the other alternatives cited?

The answer is that businesses, represented by common stocks, create the wealth of an advanced economy. Bond interest

EXHIBIT 13–6
The Power of Compound Interest (Starting with $100,000,)

Years Compounding	Compounding Rate		
	5%	9.85%	15%
5	$128,000	$ 160,000	$ 201,000
15	208,000	409,000	814,000
30	432,000	1,675,000	6,621,000
45	899,000	6,855,000	53,877,000

is paid by the cash flow of businesses and government bond interest is paid by taxes on business wealth. Real estate rents are paid by business cash flow. Art, commodities, and precious metals are purchased with wealth produced by businesses. It follows then that businesses, over the long term, must produce higher returns than expenses, that is, bonds, art, commodities, real estate, and precious metals.

IMPORTANCE OF TIME

Nothing is more important in life and nothing is more important in investments than time—yet time seems to be glossed over in so many things and by so many people.

Although time was spoken of a chapter earlier, perhaps the subject can be readdressed for the chart above that effectively demonstrates the power of compound interest over a period of time.

Over a 45-year working lifetime, the difference between compounding at 5 percent and 9.85 percent is $6 million or 7.6 times as much. The difference between 9.85 percent and 15 percent—the minimum potential for value investors—is $47 million. Perhaps tolerating price fluctuations in equities over a lifetime is worth it.

EFFECTS OF INFLATION

Remember 1982, when economists assured us that Paul Volcker had twisted the tail of inflation and killed it dead? That belief

EXHIBIT 13-7
Returns Required to Maintain Purchasing Power of Capital

Inflation	Tax Bracket					
Rate	*25%*	*30%*	*35%*	*40%*	*45%*	*50%*
8%	10.7	11.4	12.3	13.3	14.5	16.0
9	12.0	12.9	13.8	15.0	16.4	18.0
10	13.3	14.3	15.4	16.7	18.2	20.0
11	14.7	15.7	16.9	18.3	20.0	22.0
12	16.0	17.1	18.5	20.0	21.8	24.0
13	17.3	18.5	20.0	21.6	23.6	26.0
14	18.6	20.0	21.5	23.3	25.5	28.0
15	20.0	21.4	23.1	25.0	27.2	30.0

Source: *From Contrarian Investment Strategy: The Psychology of Stock Market Success* by David Dreman. Copyright ©1979 by David Dreman. Reprinted by permission of Random House, Inc.

proved greatly exaggerated. As long as Americans—people, businesses, and governments—borrow and spend excessively, putting pressure on the Fed to increase the money supply, we remain on course for more inflation and high interest rates.

Inflation has always been here. However, at this time, it might serve to point out that inflation is strictly a monetary phenomenon. The American public has never had the political discipline to keep it in check. Inflation has been likened to living in a country where nobody speaks the truth. Has the problem disappeared? Hardly. Consumer prices in 1987 rose at a 4.41 percent annual pace. That obliterated any real aftertax returns from holding T-bills.

What does this mean to you as an investor? Put simply, as an investor you face a tax structure that punishes increasingly as the rate of inflation soars. If inflation reignited at the 13.4 percent of 1979, investors ensconced in a 33 percent tax bracket would require a 20 percent return just to sustain purchasing power. Exhibit 13–7 shows that given high, but not impossible, inflation levels, the returns required become frightening.

CONCLUSION

Chapter 13 presents solid evidence of the exceptional performance of stocks over the long haul, as compared with other financial mechanisms. Also introduced was the efficacy of time and the power it brings to long-term thinking.

Some of the greatest opportunities in decades presently await prudent, cautious investors. What is important is to keep repeating the words of Bernard Baruch, quoted in the introduction: *two and two equals four*. The value investor should perhaps constantly keep that in mind when mingling with Wall Street.

NOTES

1. Henry R. Oppenheimer, "A Test of Ben Graham's Stock Selection Criteria," *Financial Analysts Journal*, Sept.–Oct. 1984, p. 68.
2. Henry R. Oppenheimer, "Ben Graham's Net Current Asset Values: A Performance Update," *Financial Analysts Journal*, Nov.–Dec. 1986, p. 40.

CHAPTER 14

WHICH WAY TO INVEST?

Having developed goals and objectives, the investor must decide how to implement the value philosophy outlined in this book.

Value investing can be approached through a variety of methods, none better than the other. The different approaches simply reflect different personal and investing philosophies and strategies.

METHODS OF INVESTING

This chapter addresses some of the practical aspects, from the nitty-gritty of doing it yourself to the prospect of employing an investment adviser plus the way to obtain the best results. Listed here are four methods of investing:

1. Do it yourself.
2. Use the services of a stockbroker.
3. Invest in mutual funds.
4. Hire an investment adviser.

A tangential method could be to combine two or more approaches such as personally managing part of the value portfolio and purchasing appropriate mutual funds with the remainder. Or, if the asset base is large enough, the investor could split funds between a stockbroker and investment adviser for purposes of comparison.

No matter which way the investor determines, adequate monitoring must be maintained in order to keep on top of a value program.

Investing on Your Own

Investing on your own is practically a full-time occupation. Do-it-yourselfers must uncover their own investment possibilities, do their own research as well as their own buys and sells, and monitor portfolio performance. Ideally, do-it-yourselfers should have some experience in investing and have some accounting and financial know-how. Under those conditions, a do-it-yourselfer with some ability could probably achieve better returns than most pros.

The value investor planning to act independently should plan to spend at least 25 to 30 hours a week on investing. The investor should also subscribe to numerous publications (scan some in the public library) and send for corporate, annual, and quarterly reports to use in research.

Several statistical services that are handy were previously indicated; some are publications while others are computer databases. For the latter, a personal computer is a necessity along with appropriate accessories. Such a setup permits the investor to research all database stocks for interesting value possibilities which then must be followed up.

The investor could consider use of a discount broker or a full service broker who'll do business at discount rates. Although value investors rarely trade extensively, money saved in commission costs earns that much more in current income and capital appreciation.

Finally, the investor should set a target sell price on each security. When any issue reaches its predesignated price, it should be sold unless company fundamentals indicate the sell price should be changed.

Using a Stockbroker

Some stockbrokers specialize in value investing and do value research very well. Several large brokerage firms have created separate value research arms as well. These brokers and firms are worth searching out. One caveat: the investor shouldn't operate blindly. Operations should be monitored to be sure the value philosophy remains consistent and absolute.

Using Value Mutual Funds

Value mutual funds, another alternative, provide diversification and professional money management not otherwise available to the smaller or average-sized accounts.

Of course, the investor pays for these advantages. Management fees run around .75% of mutual fund assets. This, plus other miscellaneous costs, may boost annual expenses to well over 1% of assets. Be careful, also, of 12b(1) fees, which are extra fees some funds charge for marketing expense.

What should an investor look for in a fund? Research those with a well-defined long-term value philosophy, continuity of management, and good long-term performance record.

What are the drawbacks? Mainly the lack of personal touch. Portfolios can't be tailored to special preferences and needs.

Hire an Investment Manager

Managing a value-investment program requires considerable attention to detail, time, experience, and hard work. This makes it no different than other professional endeavors where superior long-term results are demanded.

Private individuals can and do succeed, given proper training and experience. But investors usually make the money they have for investing in other fields or businesses. The specialized attributes that build wealth in a manufacturing enterprise or a medical practice are not the same as the specialized ones needed for investing.

For those reasons, many investors might consider the services of a professional advisory firm the most appropriate way to invest. The adviser carries out the day-to-day work, following a philosophy and plan the investor directs.

If the investor seeks that route, keep in mind that most effective money management firms specialize in a particular philosophy, be it value equities, growth stocks, small capitalized issues, and so forth. Look for a firm whose philosophy most closely conforms to the investor's—a philosophy that permits a degree of comfort. Then calmly, over the long-term, the investor and adviser will work together to execute an investment plan.

In other words, the selection process works like this: philosophy first, adviser second. You don't pick out your adviser and then inquire as to her or his investment philosophy.

Even here a word of caution is necessary: Do not hire an adviser simply because of a sales pitch. The adviser must work for and satisfy the investor.

A particular adviser, for example, may be successful and hold a long-term superior record of purchasing low P/E, small businesses that have escaped the attention of most investors. That sounds good, but the adviser isn't going to work in a vacuum. Suppose the investor's father had invested considerable funds in a small company in 1955 and the investment hadn't panned out, causing personal difficulties.

In that case, the investor might be psychologically unprepared for a program geared toward investing in small, unknown, companies—especially in periods of market declines.

Perhaps a manager who sticks to low P/E, large "blue chip" businesses would really be more suited to administer such an investor's plan. The latter would have a philosophy that particular investor could wholeheartedly stick with without being derailed at critical points.

Once a competent adviser has been selected, the investor still has a job to do. Good clients make great firms. In other words, clients who do their part help the firm's success and thereby their own.

How to Get the Most from an Investment Adviser

The first way in which an investor can be a good client is to understand the adopted philosophy, including the philosophical implications for potential long-term results, short-term results, and emotional and economic difficulties.

For example, the Graham & Dodd value philosophy usually means the purchase of unpopular securities. Bargain levels are difficult to find in securities whose prices are actively moving up, that are the "talk of Wall Street," or that are well recognized as superior businesses.

Therefore, an initial value portfolio, unless purchased just before the commencement of a bull market, may likely be unexciting. Unpopular securities do not become optative over-night; usually it takes up to three years before a value portfolio begins to demonstrate its initial intrinsic worth.

Monitor the construction of the portfolio, making certain the adviser has stuck to the agreed on philosophy. Do not, however, get caught up in the minutiae. ("Minutiae" to a value-investor includes the requests for short-term interim quotes, or even monthly portfolio evaluations.)

If questions arise about particular issues, focus the discussion on how the issue relates to the chosen philosophy and whether the adviser is still "on track."

The investor's second responsibility as a client is to communicate. Tell the investment adviser the amount of money available for equity investments, how much will be available in the future, and the time horizon. Keep the adviser informed of any changes that might affect that plan. Large, unexpected, capital withdrawals can disturb investing strategies, especially during market lows. Finally, let the adviser know of concerns or problems that might affect a long-term contract.

Doing your part can save you not only considerable money but also great frustration, not to mention hard feelings, if problems arise. Changing advisers can be costly, setting back an investment plan and increasing the amount of time required for the plan to prove itself. Additionally, changing advisers can result in significant transaction costs as one adviser's positions are sold and another's purchased.

CHAPTER 15

THE SUMMING UP

At the beginning of this book I discussed three ingredients necessary for successful investing in businesses. They were knowledge, correct action, and patience. Even with these ingredients you can't win all the time, but you can have a high batting average.

Patience is often the key to success whether the asset is stocks or real estate or a business. Don't expect to gain financial success overnight. Times will come when stocks aren't performing satisfactorily. That's when patience must be exercised. Don't fidget. Don't fuss. Don't be concerned with day-to-day market fluctuations. The business cycle hasn't been either conquered or even leashed.

Moreover, new factors have not changed the basic principles and tools of successful value investment. Throughout the preceding pages, attempts have been made to show what these basic principles and tools are, and how to use them to determine what type of stock to buy, when to buy it, and when to sell. But, knowing and understanding these rules aren't enough unless the investor also has patience and self-discipline.

Throughout *Value Investing Today,* rules have been supplied which should eliminate crucial errors and at the same time provide opportunities for significant gains.

Why invest now? a reader might ask.

We live at a time when the human race may advance more than ever before in history. The investment risks of the last few years have been substantial. However, the records for the successful have been even more substantial. But the investment rewards of the past 50 years may pale beside those of the next 50.

The purpose of this book, again, is to try to show an investor how to capture those rewards.

The strategies put forth are relatively simple: They require some time to learn and to capitalize on effectively. However, no investment strategy should be followed blindly. This is why much of this book has been devoted to explaining why the methods work.

A last caveat: Conventional opinion almost always advocates the popular course. But the reader has already seen the "Street" is oriented towards short-term results and instant gratification.

As an investor, you must steel yourself to stand apart and defy group thinking. Most successful value investors are individualists who have chosen their own paths. So, while the rest of the world rushes to buy great concepts or the latest high flyer, the successful value investor must hang tough and stick to basics. If you do, I believe you will have a markedly better chance of improving investment performance. All that's required is a disciplined mind, the courage of your convictions and patience. If you have these qualities, I believe you will find investing in businesses throughout the world a rewarding pursuit.

INDEX